THE NEW BEST OF FINE WOODWORKING

Traditional
Finishing
Techniques

Traditional Finishing Techniques

The Editors of
Fine Woodworking

The Taunton Press

The Taunton Press, Inc., 63 South Main Street, PO Box 5506, Newtown, CT 06470-5506
e-mail: tp@taunton.com

Distributed by Publishers Group West

Jacket/Cover design: Susan Fazekas
Interior design: Susan Fazekas
Layout: Susan Lampe-Wilson
Front and Back Cover Photographer: Mark Schofield

The New Best of Fine Woodworking® is a trademark of The Taunton Press, Inc.,
registered in the U.S. Patent and Trademark Office.

Library of Congress Cataloging-in-Publication Data
Traditional finishing techniques / The editors of Fine woodworking.
     p. cm. -- (The new best of fine woodworking)
  ISBN 1-56158-733-8
  1. Wood finishing. I. Fine woodworking. II. Series.
  TT325.T73 2004
  684'.084--dc22

                    2004006905

Printed in the United States of America
10 9 8 7 6 5 4 3 2 1

The following manufacturers/names appearing in *Traditional Finishing Techniques* are trademarks: 3M®,
Adalox®, Antiquax®, BASF®, Bear-Tex®, Benjamin Moore®, Bioshield™, Bondo®, Chinex®, Deft®,
Diamond Grit®, Durite®, Formby's®, Grumbacher®, Hermes®, Imperial®, Liberon®, Livos®, Makita®,
Mazola®, Meguiar's®, Metalite®, Minwax®, Mohawk®, No-Fil®, Norton®, Norzon®, Old Masters®,
Philips®, Porter Cable®, Powerkut®, Pratt & Lambert®, Production®, Purdy®, Regalite®, Scotch-Brite®,
SealCoat®, Sherwin Williams®, Sherwin-Williams®, Stanley®, Syntox®, Three-M-ite®, Transtint®
Tri-M-ite®, Tynex®, Viva®, Walgreens®, Watco®, Waterlox®, Winsor & Newton®, Zinsser®

Working wood is inherently dangerous. Using hand or power tools improperly or ignoring safety
practices can lead to permanent injury or even death. Don't try to perform operations you learn about
here (or elsewhere) unless you're certain they are safe for you. If something about an operation doesn't
feel right, don't do it. Look for another way. We want you to enjoy the craft, so please keep safety
foremost in your mind whenever you're in the shop.

Acknowledgments

Special thanks to the authors, editors, art directors, copy editors, and other staff members of *Fine Woodworking* who contributed to the development of the articles in this book.

Contents

Introduction

After cutting, shaping and joining wood comes finishing, and with it, a sense of anxiety. If the finish is botched, all the work that went before is for nothing. Small wonder many woodworkers find a reliable method and stick with it. That's part of the reason why traditional finishes are still widely used by woodworkers and finishers. Oil finishes, varnishes, and shellac are relatively easy to apply, and they give consistent results.

A well finished piece of furniture sings. A gleaming varnish that pops the grain commands attention. A hand-rubbed oil finish has so much depth that it begs to be touched. Shellac has been used for centuries, and for period furniture, it has no peer. Even humble wax can impart a mellow glow that enhances as it protects.

For all the beauty these time-tested finishes offer, using them requires relatively little investment in tools and materials. You don't need expensive spray equipment or a compressor to apply traditional finishes. A good brush or even a rag will do. Learning to get good results with these methods is where the investment comes in. Some finishes, such as wipe-on oil finishes, are almost fool proof. Others like brushing glossy varnish or French polishing take some patience to develop the knack.

These articles from *Fine Woodworking* have been selected to help you master these time-tested techniques. You'll learn how to prepare wood for a flawless finish, color wood to pop grain and match finishes, use a brush properly, and pad on shellac. Traditional finishers like to come up with their own brews, and we offer a few recipes to inspire your own creativity.

We've also included information on using traditional finishes in restoring period furniture. Not only will the advice from these experienced woodworkers and finishers help you get the finish you want, getting there might be just a little less stressful.

—Helen Albert
Executive Editor, Taunton Books

Making Sense of Sandpaper

BY STROTHER PURDY

Years ago at a garage sale, I bought a pile of no-name sandpaper for just pennies a sheet. I got it home. I sanded with it, but nothing came off the wood. Sanding harder, the grit came off the paper. It didn't even burn very well in my woodstove.

Sanding is necessary drudge work, improved only by spending less time doing it. As I learned, you can't go right buying cheap stuff, but it's still easy to go wrong with the best sandpaper that's available. Not long ago, for example, I tried to take the finish off some maple flooring. Even though I was armed with premium-grade, 50-grit aluminum-oxide belts, the work took far too long. It wasn't that the belts were bad. I was simply using the wrong abrasive for the job. A 36-grit ceramic belt would have cut my sanding time substantially.

The key to choosing the right sandpaper is knowing how the many different kinds of sandpaper work. Each component, not just the grit, contributes to the sandpaper's performance, determining how quickly it works, how long it lasts, and how smooth the results will be. If you know how the components work together, you'll be able to choose your sandpaper wisely, and use it efficiently. Then you won't waste time sanding or end up burning the stuff in your woodstove.

Sandpaper Is a Cutting Tool

What sandpaper does to wood is really no different from what a saw, a plane or a chisel does. They all have sharp points or edges that cut wood fibers. Sandpaper's cutting is simply on a much smaller scale. The only substantial difference between sandpaper and other cutting tools is that sandpaper can't be sharpened.

Look at sandpaper up close, and you'll see that the sharp tips of the abrasive grains look like small, irregularly shaped sawteeth (see the drawing on p. 9). The grains are supported by a cloth or paper backing and two adhesive bonds, much the way that sawteeth are supported by the sawblade. As sandpaper is pushed across wood, the abrasive grains dig into the surface and cut out minute shavings, which are called swarf in industry jargon. To the naked eye, these shavings look like fine dust. Magnified, they look like the shavings produced by saws or other cutting tools (see the inset photo at right).

Even the spaces between the abrasive grains serve an important role. They work the way gullets on sawblades do, giving the shavings a place to go. This is why sandpaper designed for wood has what's called an open coat, where only 40% to 70% of the backing is covered with abrasive. The spaces in an open coat are hard to see in fine grits but are very obvious in coarse grades.

Closed-coat sandpaper, where the backing is entirely covered with abrasive, is not appropriate for sanding wood because the swarf has no place to go and quickly clogs the paper. Closed-coat sandpaper is more appropriate on other materials such as steel and glass because the particles of swarf are much smaller.

WHAT GOES ON BETWEEN BELT SANDER AND BOARD?
Sandpaper is a kind of cutting tool, like a saw or a plane. Magnified (inset photo), swarf from sanding with the grain looks like shavings from a ripsaw.

DISKS DON'T FLEX, THEY BREAK.
The adhesive and backing on a random-orbit sanding pad can crack if the disk is folded like ordinary sandpaper.

At each step, you simply erase the scratches you made previously with finer and smaller scratches until, at 180 grit or 220 grit, the scratches are too small to see or feel. But there are a fair number of opinions on how to do this most efficiently.

Don't skip grits, usually Skipping a grit to save time and sandpaper is a common temptation, but not a good idea when working with hardwoods. You can remove the scratches left by 120-grit sandpaper with 180 grit, but it will take you far more work than if you use 150 grit first. You will also wear out more 180-grit sandpaper, so you don't really save any materials. When sanding maple, for instance, skipping two grits between 80 and 180 will probably double the total sanding time. This, however, is not as true with woods such as pine. Softwoods take much less work overall to sand smooth. Skipping a grit will increase the work negligibly and may save you some materials.

Sand bare wood to 180 or 220 grit
For sanding bare wood, 180 grit will generally give you a surface that looks and feels perfectly smooth and is ready for a finish of some kind. Sanding the surface with a finer grit is only necessary if you're going to use a water-based finish. These finishes will pick up and telegraph the smallest scratches. Sanding the wood to 220 grit or finer will prepare the surface better. However, it's not always wise to sand to a finer grit. You will waste your time if you can't tell the difference, and you may create problems in finishing. Maple sanded to 400 grit will not take a pigmented stain, for example. Pigments work by lodging themselves into nooks and crannies on the surface; without them, pigments will have no place to stick.

Sand faster across the grain How many times have you been told never to sand across the grain? True enough. The scratches are much more obvious, look terrible and

Some sandpaper is advertised as non-loading, or stearated. These papers are covered with a substance called zinc stearate—soap, really—which helps keep the sandpaper from clogging with swarf. Stearated papers are only useful for sanding finishes and resinous woods. Wood resin and most finishes will become molten from the heat generated by sanding, even hand-sanding. In this state, these substances are very sticky, and given the chance, they will firmly glue themselves to the sandpaper. Stearates work by attaching to the molten swarf, making it slippery, not sticky, and preventing it from bonding to the sandpaper.

Methods for Sanding Efficiently

Sanding a rough surface smooth in preparation for a finish seems a pretty straight-forward proposition. For a board fresh out of the planer, woodworkers know to start with a coarse paper, perhaps 80 grit or 100 grit, and progress incrementally without skipping a grade up to the finer grits.

are hard to remove with the next finer grit. But what holds true for planing wood is also true for sanding. You will plane and sand faster and more easily when the direction of your cuts is between 45° and 60° to the grain, because the wood-fiber bundles offer the least resistance to the cutting edges. Cross-grain scratches are harder to remove simply because they are deeper.

Use a combination of cross-grain and with-grain sanding to get the smoothest surface in the fastest manner. First make passes at 45° to 60° to both the left and the right, making an X-pattern on the workpiece. Then, with the same grit, sand with the grain to remove the cross-grain scratches. Do this with each grit when belt-sanding and hand-sanding. The non-linear sanding action of random-orbit and orbital sanders can't take advantage of the wood's grain properties. When I use my orbital, I just sand with the grain.

Choosing From the Four Abrasive Minerals

Four common abrasive minerals are aluminum oxide, silicon carbide, ceramics, and garnet. Except for garnet, they are all manufactured, designed if you will, for different cutting properties. Harder and sharper minerals cut deeper scratches and, consequently, sand the wood faster. But these deep scratches leave a coarse finish, whether you sand with or across the grain.

Softer minerals within the same grit size will cut far more slowly but leave a smoother finish. For example, if you sand a board on one side with a 120-grit ceramic, the hardest abrasive mineral, and the other side with 120-grit garnet, the softest, you will be able to feel a distinct difference between the surfaces. It will seem as if you sanded the two sides with different grit sizes.

It's easy to rate each mineral's hardness and sharpness, but it's not as simple to prescribe specific uses beyond generalizations.

Abrasive Grading Systems

The most common grading systems used in North America are CAMI, FEPA and micron grading. CAMI and FEPA are similar in grades up to about 220. Beyond that, they diverge greatly.

The three systems grade particle size to different tolerances but by the same methods. From the coarsest grits up to about 220, particles are graded through a series of wire mesh screens. The smaller grit sizes are graded through an air- or water-flotation process that separates particles by weight.

CAMI-GRADED ABRASIVES tolerate the widest range of particle sizes but are perfectly good for sanding wood.

P-GRADED ABRASIVES are to tighter tolerances than the CAMI grades.

MICRON-GRADED ABRASIVES are most uniform in size and best for sanding finishes.

CAMI (U.S. Std.)	FEPA (P-scale)	FEPA (P-scale)
		5
1,200		
		9
1,000		
800		
		15
	1,200	
600		
	1,000	
500		
		20
	800	
400		
	600	
360		
		30
	500	
	400	
320		
		40
	360	
280		
		45
	320	
		50
	280	
240	240	
	220	60
220		
180	180	
		80
150		
	150	
		100
120	120	
100		
	100	150
80	80	180
	60	
60		
	50	
50		
40	40	
36	36	
30	30	
24		
	24	
20		
	20	
16		

(Column at center labeled top to bottom: Finishing, Smoothing, Shaping)

The chart on p. 7 is helpful in comparing grits of the three grading systems, but it doesn't tell the whole story. Abrasives on the P-scale are graded to tighter tolerances than CAMI-graded abrasives. This means that the CAMI-scale tolerates a wider range of grain sizes within the definition of 180 grit than the P-scale. Tolerances are even tighter for micron grading. P-graded and micron-graded abrasives give more consistent cuts with fewer stray scratches from outsized minerals.

Micron-graded abrasives on polyester films are about three times as expensive as paper products and probably not worth it for sanding wood. I have a hard time telling the difference between wood sanded with a 100μ finishing film abrasive and standard 120-grit sandpaper. But for polishing a high-gloss finish, I find micron-graded abrasives make a substantial difference.

There are many other factors that influence the appropriateness of a sandpaper for a job.

Some Fine Points About Grading Scales

If you don't mind that we have two measurement systems, the U.S. Customary (foot, gallon) and the International (meter, liter), then you won't mind that we have three major abrasive grit-grading systems. In North America, the Coated Abrasives Manufacturers Institute (CAMI) regulates the U.S. Standard Scale. CAMI-graded sandpapers simply have numbers, such as 320, printed on them. The Europeans have the P-scale, regulated by the Federation of European Producers Association (FEPA). These abrasives are identifiable by the letter P in front of the grit size, such as P320. Finally, to make sure everyone is really confused, there is a totally different micron grading system. This system is identified by the Greek letter mu, as in 30μ.

The Supporting Role of Backings and Bonds

The backing's stiffness and flatness influence the quality and speed of the sandpaper's cut. For the most part, manufacturers choose adhesives and backings to augment the characteristics of a particular abrasive grit. You will have a hard time finding an aggressive abrasive mineral, for example, on a backing suited to a smooth cut.

The stiffer the paper, the less the abrasive minerals will deflect while cutting. They will cut deeper and, consequently, faster. Soft backings and bonds will allow the abrasives to deflect more, giving light scratches and a smooth finish. You must even consider what's behind the backing. Wrapping the sandpaper around a block of wood will allow a faster cut than sanding with the paper against the palm of your hand. For instance, an easy way to speed up your orbital sander is by exchanging the soft pad for a stiff one (see the photo on the facing page). The other consideration

Sandpaper in Cross Section

Sandpaper is made of abrasive minerals, adhesive and a cloth, paper or polyester backing. The abrasive minerals are bonded to the backing by two coats of adhesive; first the make coat bonds them to the backing; then the size coat locks them in position.

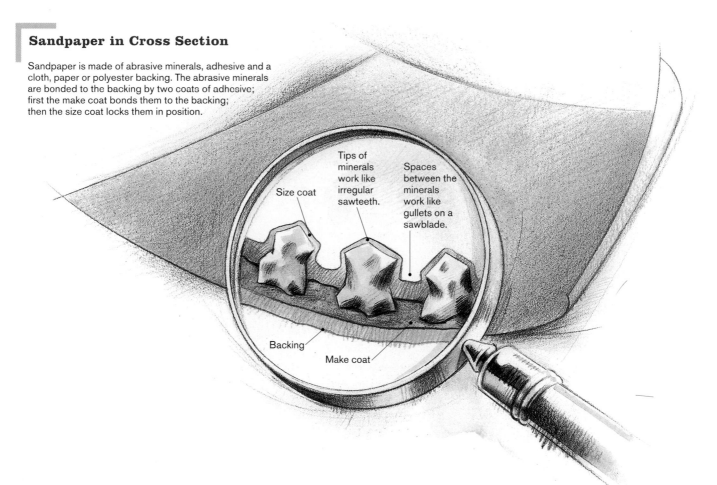

Tips of minerals work like irregular sawteeth.

Spaces between the minerals work like gullets on a sawblade.

Size coat

Backing

Make coat

is the flatness of the backing, which has nothing to do with its stiffness. Flat backings position the minerals on a more even level so they cut at a more consistent depth, resulting in fewer stray scratches and a smoother surface.

Cloth is the stiffest but least-flat backing. It will produce the coarsest and fastest cut. Cloth comes in two grades, a heavy X and a light J. Paper is not as stiff as cloth but it's flatter. It comes in grades A, C, D, E, and F (lightest to heaviest). An A-wt. paper that has been waterproofed is approximately equivalent to a B-wt. paper, if one existed. Polyester films, including Mylar, look and feel like plastic. They are extremely flat and pretty stiff. They will give the most consistently even cut and at a faster rate than paper.

The backings for hand sheets and belts are designed to flex around curves without breaking. This is not true for sanding

disks for random-orbit sanders. They are designed to remain perfectly flat, and if used like a hand sheet, the adhesive will crack off in large sections (see the photo on p. 6). This is called knife-edging because the mineral and adhesive, separated from the backing, form knife-like edges that dig into and mark the work.

Adhesive bonds on modern sandpaper are almost exclusively urea- or phenolic-formaldehyde resins. Both are heat-resistant, waterproof and stiff. Hide glue is sometimes used in conjunction with a resin on paper sheets. It is not waterproof or heat-resistant, but hide glue is cheap and very flexible.

STROTHER PURDY is a former assistant editor of *Fine Woodworking* magazine.

Sanding in Stages

BY GARY STRAUB

Everything from sharp stones to sharkskin has been used to smooth wood. Today there's a seemingly endless array of sanding tools, aids and abrasives available, all designed to make our work faster, easier, and better. If we look back at the methods used to smooth wood, we should appreciate the ease with which we can produce results far superior to those of our predecessors. Even so, most woodworkers still dread sanding.

That's too bad because sanding is one of the most important aspects of producing a fine piece. No matter how much time and care go into the making of a piece, its overall beauty is in large measure determined by how well it's been sanded. Although some finish representatives will tell you differently, no finish can cover up a mediocre sanding job.

Sanding doesn't have to be sheer drudgery, however, if you break the job down into its various stages and integrate the smoothing process with the construction of a piece of furniture. Before I've even ripped a board to width or crosscut it to length, I've belt-sanded it to 100-grit. I remove all flaws with this preliminary sanding so that the only reason for further sanding is to remove the scratches created by the previous coarser grit. By the time I glue-up, everything's been sanded to 150 grit, which makes post-assembly sanding a breeze.

The result of this division of labor is a better sanding job, less tedium and a finer finished piece. The sanding system I've developed over the past 20 years of furniture making takes advantage of a wide range of abrasive materials. But before I explain my techniques, let's look at what's available today.

The Materials

Sandpaper was invented when someone figured out how to glue screened particles of glass or sand onto a paper backing. Today, of course, true sandpaper and glasspaper are practically unavailable. They have been replaced by papers that use much harder and sharper minerals, both natural and synthetic. New abrasive materials, more sophisticated screening methods, and superior papers and glues have transformed the ways we smooth wood. Not long ago, abrasives came in grits from 12 to 600; now they go into the thousands (see the photo on p. 12). As if that weren't enough, we also have steel wool, abrasive cloths, pads, powders, liquids, and pastes. Knowing what to use has become a challenge.

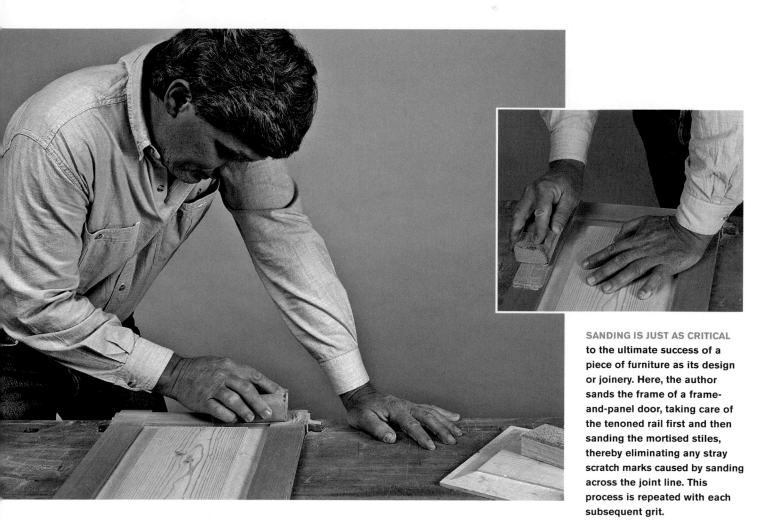

SANDING IS JUST AS CRITICAL to the ultimate success of a piece of furniture as its design or joinery. Here, the author sands the frame of a frame-and-panel door, taking care of the tenoned rail first and then sanding the mortised stiles, thereby eliminating any stray scratch marks caused by sanding across the joint line. This process is repeated with each subsequent grit.

Abrasives In ascending order of hardness, the materials used for coated abrasives are glass, silica sand, garnet, aluminum oxide, silicon carbide, and zirconia alumina. The abrasive is applied to a backing as an open or closed coat. A closed coat means there is complete coverage while an open coat has 40% to 60% coverage. Closed-coat abrasives are more aggressive but clog easier. Open-coat abrasives are less aggressive but don't clog as easily. Most wood sanding is best done with open-coat paper, but some very hard woods can be sanded with closed coat. Wet sanding can be done with closed-coat paper (the liquid keeps the abrasive from becoming clogged).

Backing materials Backing materials come in weights from A to X, with A-wt. being the lightest. I use mostly A-wt., or finish paper, and C-wt., cabinet or production paper. A-wt. is very flexible for hand-

and finish-sanding. C-wt. is heavier but still fairly flexible for machine-sanding. Disks are often E-wt. paper, cloth-backed sheets are J-wt. and sanding belts are usually X-wt. cloth.

Bonding agents The abrasives can be bonded to the backing material with several different glues: hide glue for its flexibility, resins for their strength, or a combination of both. The grains may be electrostatically arranged, and often another coat of resin is added to maintain orientation. This is resin over resin and is used on better sanding belts and in other applications where strength of bond is more important than flexibility.

Reading the paper Each company has its own method of displaying product information on the back of the sheets of sandpaper (see photo p. 13). The type of abrasive

is often written out fully (aluminum oxide or garnet, for example). The grit is displayed by a number, sometimes preceded by a letter, such as P100, and the coating may either be written out fully or abbreviated (Open Coat or OP). The backing weight may be shown as A or A-wt., or combined with either the grit designation (120A) or the information on coating density (AOP).

Choosing a paper Generally, I use aluminum oxide papers with my portable sanding machines and switch to garnet for hand-sanding. Aluminum oxide lasts longer because it's a lot harder than garnet and so is more suited to machine sanding. It doesn't break down, however, so the sharp edges will become dull. The combination of a dull belt and the speed of the machine (especially a belt sander) can severely burnish the wood, which could affect how it finishes. Dull belts should be replaced. Garnet continuously breaks down, exposing fresh sharp edges, but because it's softer than aluminum oxide, I use it only for hand-sanding.

I sand from 80 to 220 using aluminum oxide and garnet papers but use silicon carbide for grits 240 to 320. I also use coated abrasives on occasion. These papers are often silicon carbide, coated with a material, such as zinc stearate, that prevents the papers from clogging. I've found them helpful in sanding oily or resinous woods, but (contrary to what the manufacturers will tell you) there's a possibility of the residue contaminating the finish.

Non-Paper abrasives In addition to sandpaper, I also use 3M's Scotch-Brite or Norton's Bear-Tex nylon pads and steel wool. The pads are made of abrasive-coated fibrous nylon. They're very flexible, they last much longer than steel wool and they come in different grades, from coarse to ultra-fine. They're also good for wet sanding because they're unaffected by water, oil, or solvents.

I use 00, 000 and 0000 (progressively finer) steel wool for finish work and sometimes use the coarser grades for stripping or for routine chores like metal cleaning. I like the steel wool for finish work because it cuts better than the abrasive pads, and the steel wool burnishes the wood slightly, which gives it a better sheen.

The Method

The sanding process needn't be the hassle that we often make it. I've found that sanding as I go produces better results and takes much of the monotony out of the work. I first plane or re-plane all lumber for a piece before I start. I keep my blades very sharp, and I never take more than 1/32 in. per pass. On smaller pieces, I use a handplane. Lumber planed at either the lumberyard or mill is very crudely done and of poor consistency. Trying to sand mill-planed lumber flat is a waste of time.

Using machines After planing all the lumber to a consistent thickness, I sand each piece with a portable belt sander and a 100-grit belt. This sanding is crucial because this is when I remove any flaws. It's tempting to decide that you've sanded enough and that the next grit will take care of the rest. This is never true. If you remove all the flaws on the first sanding, subsequent sandings need only remove the scratches left by the previous grit, thereby saving time overall.

Using a portable belt sander takes some practice because it's quite easy to remove far more wood than you want. Most sanders are not well-balanced, usually weighing more on one side or the other, or more toward the front or back. To compensate for this, you must exert a slight pressure opposite the weight, striving to maintain total contact with the surface. At the same time, you must keep the pressure equal in all directions. Leaning the machine to one side or the other will create long gouges. Applying too much pressure either to the front or back will cause dips.

The proper technique is to move the balanced machine back and forth slowly, with the grain, reaching comfortably but not stretching. Don't move the machine directly to the side but rather let it drift to the side as you go back and forth. Moving it sideways will cause zig-zag dips that usually remain hidden until the first coat of finish is applied.

I change belts as soon as I feel myself applying more pressure to get the belt to bite. Increasing pressure as belts dull is a primary cause of a poor sanding job. Unfortunately, the high cost of belts stimulates this bad habit. Cleaning the belt with a crepe-rubber bar belt-cleaning stick will stretch the life of your belts, but when they're dull, they're dull.

Having a brand new belt clog up with resin or glue can be very frustrating. I've had some success cleaning belts with a brass-bristled brush and in worse cases,

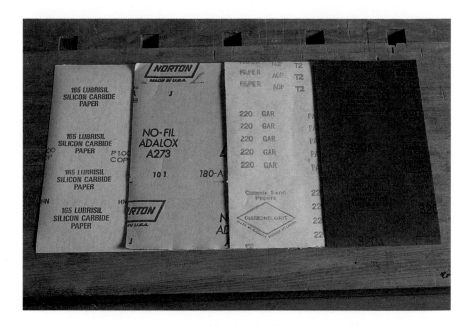

ALL YOU NEED TO KNOW ABOUT A SANDPAPER is printed on its back. Manufacturers usually indicate grit, coating density (open or closed coat), backing weight and sometimes other information, such as whether a no-clog coating has been used, as is the case with the first (Lubrisil) and second (No-Fil) sheets above.

using pitch cleaner with the brass brush. I do save all my used belts because they're still good enough for lathe work and for hand-sanding curved surfaces. I like Hermes aluminum oxide, resin-over-resin, open-coat belts. They're good belts at a fair price.

After sanding all flaws out of the lumber, I cut all stock to size, joint all the edges (finishing with a handplane), make all my joints and then dry-assemble. Next I glue up any wide panels such as tabletops. While they're drying, I sand the rest of the flat parts with a belt sander using 120 grit. All the parts that can't be sanded with a machine, I'll hand-sand with the same grit. Before sanding and between each grit, I brush each piece thoroughly to remove any residual grit—the cause of those mysterious scratches that often appear.

This sanding goes very fast, but you must be careful, especially on the edges. The only object of this sanding is to remove the previous sanding scratches because I've

FOR STRIPPING PAINT or varnish and for cleaning metal or going over a finish, steel wool and abrasive pads work better than sandpaper.

(I like Diamond Grit paper, made by the Carborundum Abrasives Co.), and then I go over all the flat surfaces before assembly. This makes problem areas—such as joints where the grain goes in different directions—much easier to deal with after assembly. I then dry-assemble the piece to check for any variation in wood thickness at the joints. Sanding these flush now makes post-assembly sanding much easier and pleasant.

When everything looks and fits right, I glue up. Because there's no turning back now, I make sure I'm satisfied that all is ready. I use glue sparingly, so there is minimum squeeze-out (but I make sure there's a little, so I know the joint isn't starved). While waiting for the glue to set, I sand any wide panels to the same 150 grit.

A good orbital sander does an excellent job of sanding, removing wood quickly while maintaining flatness. I use a Porter-Cable 505 half-sheet sander and a Makita quarter-sheet sander. I always use the largest sander that will do the job, usually the half-sheet machine. I move the machine back and forth slowly with the grain, letting the machine do the work. I apply only enough pressure to maintain control. The quickest way to ruin both furniture and machine is to apply a lot of pressure. By applying just a little more pressure on the back of the sander on the forward stroke and on the front on the return stroke, I have more control and the machine performs better.

Moving slowly is key to minimizing swirl marks because it gives the paper a chance to erase them. Just as with the belt sander, I shift sideways slowly as I'm moving back and forth to avoid creating any swirl marks, and I brush my work often to prevent pieces of grit from getting caught under the pad. On very large panels, I sand one area at a time so that I don't forget where I've been.

already removed all defects with the initial sanding. I then check for any dings that may have occurred while cutting, and if there are any, I'll put drops of water on them to raise the fibers. By this time, any wide-panel glue-ups are dry enough to remove the clamps. I use an old plane blade to remove excess glue before it dries completely; otherwise, it will lock moisture into the joints, causing problems later on.

Next, I handplane any irregularities in the glued-up surface because it's just not possible to make a large panel flat with a portable sander. Once I get the surface satisfactorily flat, I sand it with the belt sander using a 120-grit belt. I sand the back first so that I don't take a chance on scratching the top when I turn it over. I then do any decorative routing, inlays or carving, and I plane or hand-sand the panel again with 120-grit paper. Now all the pieces are made and sanded to 120 grit, which is fairly smooth.

Now I change to a half-sheet orbital sander and 150-grit aluminum oxide paper

The next step depends on the finish I'm using. I put oil on most of my work (except tabletops) because I like the way it allows the texture of the wood to be seen and felt. When finishing with oil, I stop at 150 grit. Oil is a penetrating finish, and the finer you sand, the less penetration you obtain. I apply the first coat (which does the most penetrating) before I go to finer abrasives.

For items requiring more protection, I use a surface finish such as varnish or lacquer. When I'm putting on a varnish finish, I continue machine-sanding to 220 grit and for lacquer to 320 grit.

Hand-Sanding Regardless of the finish, I always hand-sand all the pieces (except bottoms, backs, and other parts that will not show) with the same grit that I used on the last machine-sanding. This removes any remaining swirl marks and provides a good opportunity to examine every inch of the work.

Hand-sanding is labor-intensive, but it's also the most rewarding part of sanding. Using machines requires good balance and steady hands, but handwork lets you feel what you're doing. You must learn to detect slight imperfections with your hands to judge whether a curve is fair or an edge consistent.

When sanding flat surfaces by hand, you must use a sanding block to keep the surface flat (see the photo above). I prefer a solid-cork block, but I've also made sanding blocks by gluing bulletin-board cork (obtainable at most hardware stores) to a block of wood. Cork is firm enough to keep the paper flat and resilient enough not to destroy the paper. Some prefer felt- or rubber-faced sanding blocks. What's important is that you not use a block of wood alone, or it will quickly destroy the paper. The block I use takes a quarter sheet of paper.

ALWAYS SAND WITH A CUSHION to keep your surface flat. Cork blocks, cork-faced blocks and rubber sanding pads all will work. The rubber Tadpoles (right, background) allow sanding of concave and convex moldings, and the finger rubbers protect the fingers while providing a good grip on the sandpaper. The solid wood block is useful as a backing for the nylon abrasive pads.

I apply firm pressure to the block, stroking back and forth, carefully following the curves of the grain. I'm very careful with edges and corners, taking care not to round them off or taper them. If they're square, I try to keep them sharp for now. For miters, I hold the block at the same angle as the joint and sand up to the intersection from each direction. I deal with right-angle joints by sanding the tenoned section first. Then, when sanding the mortised section, I can remove any stray scratches.

Overexertion quickly leads to a hurry-up and get-it-done attitude. I take my time as if I were cutting feather-thin dovetails, sanding a small portion at a time and stopping often to brush away any loose grits. I check my progress frequently, using my bare hand to tell me where I need to sand a little more. When I finish one section, I dust thoroughly, wipe with a soft clean cloth and then feel the surface again, making sure it's right.

The last step is to eliminate any sharp edges that I've left. Using the finest grit I've sanded with to this point, I go over the edges by hand, without a pad. I twist my hand slightly as I'm moving forward, which softens the edge more quickly than if I kept

my hand fixed, and prevents the edge from
getting stuck in a groove in the paper. A
very light touch will produce a corner that
cannot be duplicated by any machine. A
little more pressure will yield a ¹⁄₁₆-in. radius
in no time.

Sanding irregular surfaces

Sanding curved pieces is much the same
as sanding flat surfaces except you have to
begin hand-sanding right from the start. A
flexible sanding block is important; I use
rubber sanding pads, varying in firmness.
Their flexibility allows them to bend to fit
most curves.

For smaller curves and for sanding on
the lathe, I tear a strip of whatever size I
need from a used sanding belt I've saved.
The heavy cloth back of the belt is pliable
enough to fit the curve yet firm enough to
maintain the shape. For small concave
shapes, such as on moldings, I cut a piece of
dowel that fits the groove and wrap it with
A-wt. paper.

I also use rubber Tadpole Contour
Sanding Grips (available from many mail-

order woodworking catalogs). They come
in various diameters, both concave and
convex, and the flat grip section is shaped at
the top to allow sanding in tight places.
They come in sets; some include flexible
sanding pads. They've made life easier, and
they're very inexpensive.

Carve as smoothly and crisply as possible,
so only minimal sanding is required. Carvings
present the most difficulty because any
sanding will alter the character of a carving.
If it's a geometric carving or a large in-the-
round carving, sanding with A-wt. paper
works well. For heavy carvings, without
fine detail, steel wool or abrasive pads conform well to irregular shapes. When I do a
lot of sanding with my fingers, I wear finger
rubbers (available at most office supply
stores). They're made for office workers to
flip easily through papers, but they're also
perfect for protecting fingers, and giving a
good grip on the sandpaper.

For highly detailed carvings, I use a
stiff nylon-bristled brush—shaped like a
toothbrush—and a slurry of powdered
pumice and mineral spirits. Pumice is made
from a type of lava and has been used

through the ages as an abrasive both in the solid and crushed form. Powdered pumice is graded like steel wool except in Fs instead of 0s. I use the finest grit that will work.

Smoothing the finish After I'm satisfied that everything is smooth and ready for the finish, I wipe everything down with a soft rag dampened in mineral spirits. This serves three purposes: First, it cleans any contaminants that may have gotten on the wood, especially oils from my hands or drops of sweat from working on a hot summer day. It also gives me an idea how the piece will look finished and reveals any remaining imperfections. These are far easier to deal with now than after applying a finish.

The smoothing process isn't over when the finish goes on. Each coat must be abraded slightly before the next is applied either to ensure adhesion, as with varnish to remove dust specks in lacquer, or to finish the smoothing of an oil finish. I sand varnished and lacquered surfaces with 320-grit silicon carbide paper, often with water on varnish. But for my oil finish, I use steel wool starting with 00 and changing to the next finer grade with each coat. I prefer steel wool to the nylon abrasive pads because it not only smooths the surface by abrasion but also gently burnishes the oil-filled wood, creating a higher luster and a smoother feel.

The final coat of finish must also be smoothed or polished. A slurry of rottenstone (a very finely powdered mineral) mixed either with water or paraffin oil makes an excellent polish. Mixed with water, it gives a higher polish; mixed with oil, it gives a more satin finish.

Felt is the best material for the final rubbing. Felt blocks that look like sanding blocks are available commercially, but you can also make your own. The best felt comes from old felt hats that you might find in your father's attic or in used-clothing stores.

The texture of that felt is very uniform, and it's stiff enough to use without a block for curved and carved parts. I just dip the felt in the slurry and rub with the grain. I rub with the felt by itself (no rottenstone) for oil finishes because I'm able to get the luster I want without abrasives. I rub harder and longer, though, because there's no danger of cutting through, now that the finish has become part of the wood.

There are many polishes for wood today that surpass rottenstone, so rottenstone is fading into history. Most finish companies either make a polish for their finish or recommend one. Also there are many automobile polishes that give excellent results on varnished or lacquered finishes. In fact, there are so many polishes available today that it's difficult to keep track of them all. I've been happy with Meguiar's Mirror Glaze, a brand I find at the local auto parts store. It comes in varying degrees of abrasiveness. One caveat: Be careful when using polishes on wood whose grain has not been filled. The residue of many polishes will fill the grain and dry to a very unnatural color, which is extremely difficult to remove.

The last step is to remove any remaining polish with a very soft cloth. Cotton diapers are excellent but in short supply in this disposable society. Lint-free polishing cloths are available from finish suppliers or auto parts stores. Wipe your piece down, and step back to admire a job well done.

GARY STRAUB has been building (and sanding) furniture in Columbia, Mo., for 31 years.

Sources

Sanding and other abrasive supplies are available from many general woodworking catalogs. There are also a number of companies whose specialty is abrasive products. Below are two companies that the author buys from.

Pyramid Products Co.
7440 E. 12th St.
Kansas City, MO 64126
800-747-3600

Skates Belting
321 Southwest Blvd.
Kansas City, MO 64108
800-821-5041

Surface Prep: Why Sanding Isn't Enough

BY PHILIP C. LOWE

As the knives on your jointer and planer go dull after the first few board feet, the surfaces of your boards take a turn for the worse. Instead of cutting the wood cleanly, the dull knives heat the surface and pound it into a compressed layer of fibers. Unfortunately, many woodworkers go straight to sandpaper at this point, removing just the tool marks and no more. Without slicing well below that crushed layer, they never see the full beauty of the wood. Minute characteristics, such as the pores and medullary rays, are obscured. To expose these hidden elements, the surface must be cut cleanly. One reason why antiques have such a glow is that all of the surfaces were planed and scraped.

I haven't been able to improve much on the classic methods for fine surface preparation. I still find that a sharp smoothing plane and scrapers are the most efficient tools to get the best surface. Aside from cutting quickly below that "compression layer," these tools leave a dead-flat surface and produce less dust.

The following process may seem like a lot of bother, but each stage involves only a few strokes with a well-tuned tool to remove the marks made by the previous tool. Don't get me wrong—I love the thickness planer as much as the next guy. It takes away hours of drudgery, leaving more time for joinery and ornamentation. But it's just a starting point for fine surface preparation.

PHILIP C. LOWE runs a furniture-making school in Beverly, Mass.

Step 1: Handplane All Surfaces

The process starts after the parts have been thickness-planed and the panels have been joined. Begin by planing all surfaces with a No. 4 smoother. Sharpen the blade with a slight curve over its entire width, leaving the corners about ¹⁄₆₄ in. back from the center. This crown prevents the corners from digging in. An iron that is correctly ground and properly adjusted laterally leaves a series of subtle undulations or hollows in the surface.

A handplane quickly flattens a surface, leaving it level but textured. A random-orbit sander, on the other hand, just follows the ups and downs that are already there. If you put a glossy finish on a tabletop that has gone straight from glue-up to sandpaper, be sure not to look at it in a raking light. You'll see hollows where there was planer snipe, where boards were misaligned and where the sander lingered.

Tips for Success

Adjust the frog so that its leading edge lines up evenly with the throat. If it is skewed, the blade will not project through the throat squarely. Make sure the bottom edge of the chipbreaker meets the blade cleanly. If there are any gaps, the chipbreaker will clog with shavings and prevent cutting. File and hone the chipbreaker flat along its bottom edge.

Like most surfacing tools, the handplane should be pushed in the direction of the grain but skewed slightly to create a shearing action. The cap iron should be tightened enough to keep the iron from shifting in use.

HANDPLANING IS THE MOST IMPORTANT STEP. A well-tuned smoothing plane will flatten the surface quickly and slice below the "compression layer" left by planer blades. To make the job easier, rub some paraffin on the sole and skew the plane slightly to create a shearing action.

SECURE THE BLADE TIGHTLY. Planing with the tool held at an angle puts lateral pressure on the blade and can shift it out of alignment.

A SLIGHTLY CROWNED PLANE BLADE WON'T DIG IN AT THE CORNERS. Grind and hone a gentle curve across the entire width of the blade, with the corners about ¹⁄₆₄ in. back from the center.

Step 2: Remove Tearout With a Cabinet Scraper

Even the best-tuned smoothing plane leaves undulations and tearout. These imperfections become quite apparent once a finish has been applied. The Stanley No. 80 cabinet scraper, with its 2¾-in.-wide blade, removes these textures, leaving even shallower undulations in their place while maintaining the level surface.

The blade of the cabinet scraper is tipped forward in the body of the tool at about 30°. The edge is burnished like a card scraper, but it starts out at a different angle. File a 45° bevel along its edge using a second-cut mill file, then hone it on medium and fine stones to create a sharp edge for burnishing. To create the burr, hold the blade in a vise and draw a burnisher along the edge.

BURNISH THE HOOK ONTO THE EDGE. Start with the burnisher at 45°. Then tilt it slightly toward level for subsequent strokes.

PLACE THE TOOL ON A FLAT SURFACE. Loosen the thumbscrews and let the blade drop down level with the sole. Then tighten the screws while keeping the blade in contact with the surface.

NEXT, TIGHTEN THE THUMBSCREW ON THE BACK SIDE. This bows the blade, regulating the depth of cut by making the blade protrude from the sole.

THE STANLEY NO. 80 CABINET SCRAPER REMOVES material faster and more uniformly than a card scraper. Continue until all of the handplane marks and most of the tearout are gone. Again, angle the tool for better cutting action.

Tips for Success

To prevent the sharp edge from getting nicked, place the blade in the tool by sliding it up through the throat. When setting up the tool, loosen the thumbscrew on the back of the body until there is no tension applied to the blade. Now place the body on a flat surface, let the blade drop down level with the sole and tighten the screws to hold the iron securely. Turning the thumbscrew on the back of the body bows the blade, which makes the cutting edge protrude and regulates the amount of cut.

Push the cabinet scraper along the grain, removing the undulations and tearout left by the plane. The hollows left by the No. 80 are shallow, but if a finish were applied at this stage, the unevenness of the surface would still be apparent. The card scraper is the next step.

Step 3: Hand-Scrape and Sand

USE A WIDE CARD SCRAPER TO REMOVE THE SUBTLE HOLLOWS left by the cabinet scraper and any remaining tearout. The flat blade should be bowed in the hands as it is pushed or pulled across the work. Scrape in the direction of the grain, and skew the tool slightly.

NO POWER SANDING NEEDED. Start with 120 grit. Sand evenly and use a cork-lined sanding block to maintain the flat surface.

The card, or hand, scraper cleans up nicely after the first two tools, leaving much subtler depressions. Like the cabinet scraper, this blade employs a burr as its cutting edge. However, the edges are filed and honed to 90°, leaving four square corners to be turned over into cutting hooks using a burnisher.

When this wide tool is sharpened correctly, it will surface a board quickly. It should be bowed slightly in the hands and pushed or dragged across the surface. A card scraper removes any leftover tearout or tool marks from a board, but it leaves a slightly detectable texture.

OK, Break Out the Sandpaper

To bring the panel to final smoothness, go through a few grits of sandpaper. Start with 120 grit wrapped around a block of wood that has a thin piece of fine cork glued to the surface. Be careful to make all strokes in the direction of the grain.

Next, raise the grain by wetting the surface with a damp rag. Let it dry and jump to the next grit of sandpaper (150) and continue through 180 and 220 grits.

Worth the Effort

Each of these steps is essential to the process, and together they will produce the finest surface possible for staining and finishing. Tune up your tools, and give it a try. You will uncover a clarity in your wood surfaces that might surprise you.

RAISE THE GRAIN. After the first sanding grit, wet the surface with a damp rag and let it dry before continuing through the grits to 220.

Mix Your Own Oil Stains

BY THOMAS E. WISSHACK

I'll be the first to admit it. There's a real purity to a "natural," unstained wood finish, a real virtue to letting the wood's true figure and color come through. But if you are refinishing, restoring or reproducing a piece of furniture, well, a "natural" finish is something that you just can't afford. Color, tone and patina take years, sometimes decades, to develop on "naturally" finished pieces. In almost 20 years of refinishing and restoration work, I have developed a way to get the right color and patina in a matter of hours.

My technique for coloring wood is better than either aniline dyes or commercial stains because of the control I have over tone and depth of color. Also, the stains are largely reversible. I make my own oil stains with turpentine or paint thinner, linseed oil, Japan drier and artist's oil colors.

The turpentine serves as a solvent, diluting the pigments in the artist's oil colors; the linseed oil acts as a binder to keep the ingredients in solution; and the Japan drier ensures that the oil colors will dry within a reasonable amount of time (some dry much slower than others).

One exception is that I substitute copal painting medium (available in art-supply stores) for the linseed oil if I'm working on an antique. The reason is that linseed oil will tend to darken most woods over time. The copal works just as well as a binder. When working with an antique, I take another precautionary step. I also seal the surface prior to staining with shellac before applying any stain, so the stain can be removed entirely at a later date if more work is to be done on the piece.

The key to my stains—the secret ingredients—are the artist's oil colors. What makes them so special are the quality of the pigments used and the fineness of the grind. Artist's oil colors are generally ground much finer than the pigments used in commercial stains, which are often the same as those used in paints. Because the pigment particles are so fine, the resulting stains are much more transparent than commercial stains, letting more of the wood's figure and grain show through. And artist's oil colors are permanent and more fade-resistant than off-the-shelf wood stains.

Mixing the Stain

I mix the liquid ingredients in a glass jar. For a small batch of stain, I'll start with about a pint of turpentine or thinner, ⅓ cup linseed oil and three or four drops of the Japan drier. I mix the artist's oils separately on a small sheet of glass (my palette), and then I add the mixed pigments to the liquid mixture a little bit at a time until I get the depth of

color I'm looking for. I adjust the mix of pigments to get the tone I'm after (see the photo on p. 25).

I'm looking for a very dilute stain, on the order of a tenth or so as concentrated as a commercial product but with the consistency of low-fat (2%) milk. The advantage of such a dilute stain is that I can control it by applying it in two or three coats rather than all at once, deepening the tone while still retaining a semitransparent surface. Additionally, if the color is not quite right, I can adjust it repeatedly to alter the tone without ending up with a muddy, murky mess.

The maximum amount of artist's oils I add to the 1-pint solution is about ⅓ of a standard-size tube, or a little less than half

an ounce. This can vary, depending on the intensity of the colors used, so you'll have to experiment. But even the finest quality artist's oils will give you an opaque finish if you get too heavy-handed with them. More light coats are better than fewer heavy coats.

Because these stains are so dilute, it's rarely necessary to seal new wood prior to staining. An exception is pine, which may appear blotchy regardless of how dilute the stain is. A penetrating sealer, such as one of the commercially available Danish oil finishes or a thinned solution of tung oil, eliminates this problem.

STAIN CAN BRING OUT THE BEST. The author's table, veneered with crotch mahogany and built with cherry legs, received just one light coat of his homemade oil stain. After observing the natural colors already in the wood, he mixed a stain that accentuated them and gave the wood a head start on developing a patina.

An Endless Choice of Colors

An infinite range of color choices is one good reason to make your own oil stains. A sample board illustrates the subtle colors possible using artist's oils for your pigments:

A. The first section is natural Honduras mahogany with just one coat of linseed oil.

B. Section B has a light coat of the author's homemade oil stain applied to it. The stain consists of turpentine, linseed oil, Japan drier, and just a bit of burnt-umber oil color.

C. More umber has been added to the same stain to produce the tone in section C.

D. Cadmium red and yellow are added to the same stain to heighten the colors already in the wood.

E. Finding section D somewhat too red, the author added a little green to neutralize the red and to bring the tone back to brown.

F. A little black adds depth to the stain.

G. The mixture was thinned in half with turpentine to yield the natural-looking result in section G.

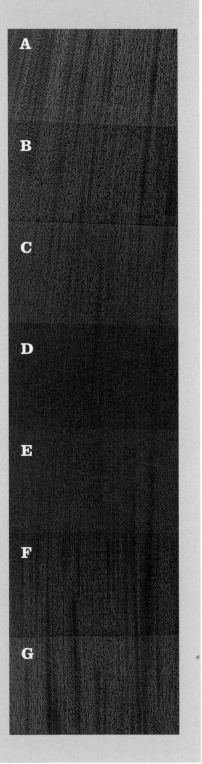

Applying the Stain

I generally brush on the first coat of my homemade stain, let it stand about 20 minutes and then wipe it off. Leaving the stain on the wood for more or less than 20 minutes will not dramatically alter the amount of color the wood absorbs but how you wipe off the stain will. A brisk rub leaves only traces of the stain on the wood's surface. Gently wiping in circles and then with the grain will leave considerably more stain on the wood. Subsequent coats can be applied with a cloth.

If you don't like the way the stain looks on the wood, usually you can remove most of it with steel wool and naphtha or paint thinner while the stain's still wet. After the wood has dried, you can try again.

Sealing in the Stain

After staining, I like to allow at least three or four days (a week is even better) before applying a finish. This allows the stain to dry thoroughly, minimizing the chance of it bleeding into the finish. An additional precaution I often take is to use a dilute coat of dewaxed (the most refined version, also called blond dewaxed) white shellac as a sealer between the stain and whatever I decide to use for a finish. The shellac will isolate the oil stain so that practically any finish can be applied without problems. Or you can just use the shellac itself as the finish.

Sometimes I'll also "spice" the white shellac with orange shellac. I add it in small increments to give the surface an amber tone that's reminiscent of an older piece. Whatever finish you use, though, be sure to refer to the can or the manufacturer's instructions to make sure it's compatible with the shellac sealer.

THOMAS E. WISSHACK makes and restores fine furniture in Galesburg, Ill.

Quick, Custom Oil Stains From Japan Colors

By Mario Rodriguez

When building an antique reproduction or re-creating a missing component, an important and difficult part of the job often can be the precise matching of the original's color. It's almost impossible to achieve this with the application of a single coat of stain even if you mix your own stains. The task often requires several coats, with successive coats used to deepen or adjust the previous application of color. My system of alternating a light coat of lacquer between coats of stain gives me unparalleled speed, flexibility, and reversibility.

For my stains, I use Japan colors suspended in turpentine. Japan colors are highly concentrated basic pigments, usually in an oil-based solution, and are available in a variety of colors. A ½ pint generally costs from $7 to $12.*

I can custom mix practically any shade I need by combining two or more colors, and I can control the intensity and opacity of the stain by varying the proportion of Japan colors to turpentine. I have used this technique to alter harsh or unnatural colors from commercial stains. Garish reds and oranges, for example, can be changed to cooler browns and rusts with a light wash of green. I've also warmed up plenty of dull gray-brown walnut pieces with a light red-orange wash.

I mix my stains by pouring a little more turpentine than I need into a glass jar, and then I add the Japan colors to the turpentine. I check the color and intensity of the stain on a sample board and adjust accordingly. Usually, I apply the color with a rag to eliminate lap marks. But I use a brush when I have to get the stain into tight areas.

After the stain is completely dry, I spray on a light coat of lacquer to act as a sealer or barrier coat. To apply the lacquer, you can use a conventional spray rig, an HVLP (high-volume, low-pressure) unit or even aerosol spray cans.

When the lacquer dries, another coat of stain can be applied to darken or change the color without disturbing the previous layer of stain. If the second coat of stain doesn't achieve the color or effect you want, simply wipe it off and try again.

MARIO RODRIGUEZ teaches woodworking in New York City, and he is a contributing editor to *Fine Woodworking* magazine, as well as the author of several books on woodworking.

* Price estimates are from 1995.

Glazes and Toners Add Color and Depth

BY DAVID E. COLGLAZIER

Many woodworkers assume they're committed to store-bought stain colors. For some finishing jobs, though, a one-time application of stain just won't do. But by adding colored finish layers at the right time, you can alter or compensate for an existing color as you go, getting exactly the right result. Two finishing products, glazes and toners, will let you do this.

Glazing and toning can add depth and color to a finish or adjust the hue to get the look you're after. I rely on both methods in my antique-restoration work because there's no other finishing process I'm aware of that can bring such subtle refinement or dimension to a finish. Despite their similarities, glazes and toners are used differently.

Glazes rely on an applicator to add texture or simulate grain detail. It helps to

GLAZING TRANSFORMS COLOR AND ADDS DETAIL. Glazes are colored finish layers applied over a sealed base, like this painted cabriole leg. Glazes stay workable long enough for blending and texturing.

think of glazing as painting (see the photo on the facing page) because you're covering, or at least partially obscuring, a base color of some kind. Glazes usually go on just before the topcoats so that you won't disturb or cover up the brush strokes.

Toners are generally not manipulated with a brush or rag after they are applied. Think of toning as applying thin layers to alter the overall color of a piece. Spraying is best.

Glazes and toners are great for refinishing, restoration, and color matching, but they aren't for every job. They require more artistic skill than other finishing methods. With glazing and toning, you need to know how to spray a finish. You often have to lock in a layer of glaze or toner by spraying a coat of nitrocellulose lacquer or shellac. If your shop isn't equipped to do this, you can use aerosol cans of lacquer (made by Deft) and shellac (Wm. Zinsser & Co.), which are readily available.

Layering Is the Key

The human eye is a very perceptive tool. With training, it can observe at least five variables of a finish: surface defects, wood-

Glossary of Common Colorants

The two most common colorants are pigments and dyes (not including substances that chemically alter wood color, such as bleaches). Pigment and dye stains can be applied to wood or as colored layers of finish.

The definitions (to simplify things, I omitted paints) presented here are partially adapted from several manufacturers' literature and from Bob Flexner's book *Understanding Wood Finishing: How to Select and Apply the Right Finish*, Rodale Press, 33 E. Minor St., Emmaus, PA 18098; 1994.

Pigments: Ground opaque particles that, when added to a binder, color wood at the surface, lodging in pores, scratches, and defects. Pigment stains vary from semiopaque to semitransparent and fade slowly. Pigments are a key ingredient in glazes.

Dyes: Tiny particles that color wood or dissolve in finish to add a transparent color layer. Dyes penetrate deeply but are known to fade. Because of their clarity, dyes offer good depth and grain readability. Dyes are often used for toning.

Stains: A broad label applied to any mixture of pigments, dyes, resins, and solvents that alters wood color. The percentage of pigment affects the clarity: Glazing and pickling stains are semiopaque, pigmented stains are semitransparent and penetrating stains are quite transparent.

Glazes: A fairly thick oil-, varnish- or water-based stain that contains pigments. Glazes are usually brushed or wiped over a sealed surface and spread or partially removed as (or just after) the thinner evaporates. Glazes are used for antiquing, coloring pores, accenting grain patterns, and adding depth to carvings and turnings.

Toners: Fast-drying solution (usually lacquer) containing dyes and/or pigments applied to a sealed surface to alter the color. Toners are sprayed on the entire surface and left to dry. Pigmented toners tend to obscure the under-color and detail; dye toners are more transparent.

Shading Stains: Designed for highlighting, shading stains are specialized toners that are applied to specific areas. They can give a shaded appearance to a surface or blend regions of color. Tinting lacquers are similar products that build quickly and are used to unify tones.

WIPING OFF A GLAZE CHANGES THE LOOK. To show how color and texture can dramatically change, the author brushes and then wipes off a burnt umber glaze on one of the oak legs. Mineral spirits or naphtha can be used to soften or remove an oil-based glaze layer. A sampling of brushes used for texturing is in the background.

GLAZES MAKE A LEG LOOK OLD. The author used glazes on three legs of a table (above) to match a leg that had darkened from iron reacting with tannin. He applied a tan base color and then defined the pores and grain patterns with darker glazes.

pore and flat-grain color, finish depth, top-coat sheen, and texture. Glazes and toners rely on the eye's ability to perceive depth. By visualizing what the final result will look like two or three steps ahead, I can plan glaze and toner layers that will compensate for or correct a hue that isn't quite right. (The sidebar on p. 31 gives a brief explanation of color matching.) Each layer, whether opaque, transparent, or somewhere in between, affects the final color, texture, and readability of the underlying wood.

Layering a finish is like building a house from the foundation up. Layers can be applied in many orders, but some are more practical than others. From the wood up, this might be a finish-layering sequence: Tint and apply pore filler, dye or stain to get the right flat-grain color, correct the hue with a toner or semitransparent glaze, lock that in with a clear layer, add a thicker glaze for texture, tone where needed to add color or shade, and put on the topcoats. Toners can be added just about anytime in the layering process to change the overall color because, usually, they are nothing more than tinted finish. However, if you want to apply a heavy, textured glaze, you typically would apply it at the end of the layering. Unlike toners that can serve as their own barrier layer, glazes always need to be topcoated.

What Are Glazes and Toners?

Glazes and toners are special stains meant to be applied over a sealed surface, rather than applied to bare wood. Glazing stains come as liquids in cans and are most often brushed or wiped on with a cloth. Toning stains come in aerosol cans (see Sources on the facing page). The pigments used as colorants in glazes make them opaque. Toners usually are a lacquer-based solution of dye and/or pigments. They're almost always thinner and more transparent than glazes, but here's where the terminology can get

Anatomy of a Layered Finish

A layered finish can add depth to a piece, adjust color, obscure or pronounce detail, add an aged look, and permit easier repair to the finish. The order of the layers can vary. The illustration shows just one example.

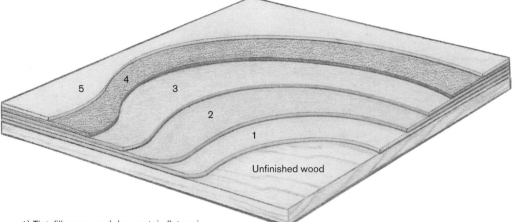

Unfinished wood

1) Tint, fill pores, and dye or stain flat grain.
2) Apply sealer (may be colored).
3) Add toning layers and barrier layers (if needed).
4) Use glazing layer for final color adjustment and surface texture.
5) Apply topcoat(s) to seal, give protection, and add sheen.

Sources

Constantine
2050 Eastchester Road
Bronx, NY 10461
800-223-8087

Liberon/Star Supply
P.O. Box 86
Mendocino, CA 95460
707-937-0375

**Mohawk Finishing
Products, Inc.**
(H. Behlen & Bros.)
Route 30 N.
Amsterdam, NY 12010
800-545-0047

**Olde Mill Cabinet
Shoppe**
1660 Camp Betty
Washington Road
York, PA 17402
717-755-8884

**Star Finishing
Products, Inc.**
360 Shore Drive
Hinsdale, IL 60521
708-654-8650

**The Woodworkers'
Store**
4365 Willow Drive
Medina, MN 55340
800-279-4441

**Woodworker's Supply,
Inc.**
1108 N. Glenn Road
Casper, WY 82601
800-645-9292

confusing. What some finishers call toner, others refer to as shading stain. Likewise, glazing is sometimes called antiquing. To distinguish some of the terms, I put together a glossary of common colorants (see the sidebar on p. 27).

Great for Restoration Jobs and Color Matching

Old finishes are not uniform. They become worn in places, faded in others. They accumulate dings, dirt, and wax from being used and polished over the years. To match the finish of an old piece of furniture, you have to fake the patina it has acquired, which can be complex. Mixing up trial stains could get you the right color, but stains ordinarily are used directly on the wood. Once applied, they are difficult to remove. By contrast, glazes and toners are layered over a sealed base (see the drawing above). Glazes can add an unusual color or mimic a grain pattern. Toners can blend in a repair, hide a wood defect or create a special effect, such as shading. I use toners more than glazes,

though I often use a combination of both in the same project.

Glazes and toners could be useful if you want to make new work look old or add a special look to a new piece, like a sunburst. Glazes and toners conceivably could give more mileage to an undesirable piece of wood. For example, a glaze could be applied to a board to simulate figure. Or, to get wider stock for a panel, you could tone the sapwood so it matches the heartwood.

To Lock in a Layer, Use a Barrier

Glazes and toners can be layered one over the other or separated by a clear film (barrier) of finish. When you don't want to disturb what's underneath, you should spray on a barrier layer. I use nitrocellulose lacquer mostly and sometimes shellac. I avoid waterborne lacquers because they can cause compatibility problems.

A barrier can lock in a layer of color and let you, with care, alter a subsequent

A GLAZE PATINA. The author applies dark glaze to a corner block for an old door frame to emphasize its age. After a light wash coat, he can dab on heavier coats in the recesses of the rosette and nail holes to simulate an accumulation of dirt.

TONING UNIFIES AN ANTIQUE SOFA TABLE. The author often tones and glazes furniture parts separately. Here, he sprays the legs and stripped table edge with a red mahogany toner. He used pigment from a can of dark stain to glaze the edges of the stretcher. The legs were wiped with this glaze, left to dry, and then shellacked.

TONER USED AS A SHADING STAIN. To simulate a table with a faded center, the author shades the edge of this mahogany top with a dark toner. After he rings the top with light, even coats, he can refine the look and color by spraying other toner bands.

layer without damaging what's under it. Lacquer barriers or lacquer-based toners can help melt one layer into the next. If a glaze layer doesn't look right, it can be removed with a rag dampened with the appropriate solvent (mineral spirits or naphtha for an oil-based glaze). Each glaze, toner, and barrier layer should be thoroughly dry before you do the next. Be especially careful when spraying lacquer over oil-based glazes because wrinkling can occur if each isn't allowed to dry thoroughly. I use several thin coats of lacquer or shellac, so any solvent will evaporate completely. Certain shellacs can introduce yellowing; however, that might be what I need to give the piece a golden, aged look.

Glazes Are Applied and Then Manipulated

Glazes develop a bite on an undercoat as the solvent evaporates, but they still offer plenty of working time (5 to 10 minutes). I apply the glaze over the surface and work it until the brush starts dragging (see the bottom photo on p. 28). This happens as the glaze turns flat. I can use a brush or rag to remove glaze from the high spots, leaving it in the recesses (see the top photo on p. 28).

Sometimes I use a dry-brushing technique, which is glazing with an almost empty brush. The bristles stay soft, not tacky or stiff as they would if the glaze were drying. Dry brushing offers the most control for putting down a minimal amount of glaze. To soften an oil-based glaze, I apply mineral spirits or naphtha after the bite occurs. This gives me a bit more time to experiment and is especially useful when I'm matching wood patterns or texture.

Viscous glazes applied over a nonporous surface can be manipulated with rags or brushes to produce special effects. Marbleizing, graining, faux-finishing, and antiquing are all forms of glazing. Glazing brushes come in an assortment of sizes and bristle types. Many finish supply stores carry a good selection of them.

I prefer oil-based glazes because of better compatibility between brands and because the solvents don't rapidly affect the previous layers I've applied. To get started, it's a good idea to practice with just a couple of glazes from one product line. Then you can expand your range with confidence. As you get better, you can use glazes in more creative ways.

Toners Are Sprayed on and Left to Dry

Toners come in many pigment and dye combinations ranging from opaque to transparent. Transparent toners can be layered to adjust color without losing the distinction between the pores and the flat grain. I probably use transparent toners the most. They're ideal for shading (see the bottom photo on the facing page) and for blending colors on components of an original piece (see the middle photo on the facing page). Using opaque toners can be like glazing. The color becomes muddier and the wood lacks grain definition, but this can be an advantage when, for example, I need to disguise a blemish. The thickness of the layer can be varied to get more opaqueness, too.

You can make your own toners by mixing dry pigments and/or alcohol-soluble aniline dyes in shellac or lacquer. For toning (shading) specific areas of furniture, I mix up a shading stain using lacquer and a low concentration of dye. I apply the shading stain in three or four thin layers so that I can sneak up on the color and not overdo it. I can always add another light layer, but if the color is too dark, it's nearly impossible to lighten uniformly. Every job hones your application skills and perception of color.

DAVID COLGLAZIER and his wife, Laurie, own and operate Original Woodworks, an antique furniture and trunk-restoration company in Stillwater, Minn.

An Endless Choice of Colors

I often have to match colors that a client or a decorator has selected. It can be tricky finishing a piece so it goes well with a rug, the wallpaper, the couch fabric, the curtains, and the other wood in the room. There are three things that make my job easier: a color wheel, stain-sample sticks, and the proper lighting.

Color correction is the art of knowing which color additives are needed to make a certain hue. For instance, red can warm up brown, and green can cool it. As simple as this sounds, the permutations of hue become far more numerous by adding black and white to darken or lighten the color.

STAIN STICKS AID COLOR CHOICES– Guided by a fan of stain sticks, the author chose a glazing stain for this tabletop. The samples also helped the customer come up with a color that makes the veneer band look natural and blend with the chair fabric.

Interestingly, men have more difficulty at color matching than women because more men have color blindness in the red and green regions of the spectrum. I don't have this problem, but even so, I still need help with color decisions. I use a primary color wheel. Grumbacher wheels (called Color Computers) are available from Star Finishing Products (see Sources on p. 29). The wheels come with directions and a summary of color theory.

Stain sticks, a collection of stir sticks that are already stained, are also helpful. The sticks (I use Old Masters brand, but you can make your own) are pinned at one end like a set of feeler gauges. I can fan them out (see the photo above) and ask the customer to determine the color direction. I don't have to make up a wall full of sample boards.

Back at the shop, I try to match colors under the same light that will be used to view the piece. True colors can change as a result of the light source. For example, incandescent light is rich in red; fluorescent light is predominantly blue. A balance of cool-white and full-spectrum fluorescent bulbs is pretty close to sunlight.

Recently, I replaced the fixtures in my shop with T8 lamps made by Philips, which use triple-phosphorous tubes. The tubes are very efficient. The light has a warm color temperature and a more natural look in the shop. They've made color matching much easier.

Dry Brushing Wood Stains

BY ROLAND JOHNSON

I pride myself on being able to restore all types of furniture. So when a customer called on me to look at two grungy, broken-down filing cabinets and asked whether I could bring them up to snuff, I couldn't say no.

The filing cabinets were made of white oak. One was missing a side; the other needed two new sides. The client liked the character of the old pieces but realized they were not valuable antiques. She wanted the repairs done for less than the cost of new

CHANGING THE COLOR OF OAK. Red oak panels in a white oak frame (above) don't match. So the author stained the piece and dry brushed the red oak to achieve a uniform color.

cabinets. We discussed options and agreed the new frames would be made of solid white oak, the panels of plywood.

I couldn't get the white oak plywood locally. With the customer's consent, I used red oak panels. I now had two finishing challenges: matching new white oak to the aged patina of the original case and making red oak look like aged white oak.

To help make these kinds of repairs appear seamless, I have developed a staining technique I call dry brushing. I've blended the light sapwood of walnut to match the dark brown heartwood. I've used it to even out hard-to-stain woods such as maple and cherry. And I can make new wood look like it's 100 years old.

Dry brushing is a two-step process that begins with traditional staining: The wood is sanded and a stain is applied and then wiped off. When that's dry, a second, heavy coat of stain is applied. This coat is delicately brushed with a soft, dry, natural-bristle brush to remove and blend any excess stain. This method leaves pigment on the surface of the wood as well as in the pores.

A Good Set of Brushes and Quality Stains and Tints

The brush must be pliable and have dense, soft bristles. I prefer natural bristles, but you could use a different kind of brush as long as it's recommended for varnish or enamel. Don't buy cheap brushes; an inexpensive brush may seem soft and supple, but it will be prone to losing bristles. It's not easy to remove bristles from a dry-brushed finish.

I keep a range of brush sizes on hand to suit different jobs. A 2-in. brush works well for small areas such as face frames and chair parts. A 2½-in. brush is good for small panels and other medium-sized surfaces. For large areas, such as tabletops, I use a 4-in. brush. This brush can really move stain around in a hurry.

APPLY A BASE COAT. The rebuilt side of the case is covered with a first coat of stain and then wiped off.

RED OAK PANELS GET SECOND COAT. Apply the blue-tinted stain to the panels; when the stain develops a dull sheen, begin dry brushing. Let the brush just skim the surface.

Color matching stains can be a real guessing game. A little knowledge about color theory will help make sense of mixing your own stains.

There are three primary colors: red, yellow, and blue. Tints are combinations of these primaries. I define tone as the shade (light or dark) of a color. Tint is the actual color.

Let's use red as an example. Red is the tint. By adding black or white, you change the tone. By adding a different color, such as blue or yellow, you change the tint. Pink is a lighter tone of red made by adding white. Purple is a new tint made by combining blue with the red. Equal amounts of all three colors produce brown.

To get specific shades of brown to match wood colors, use more or less of the primary colors. To lighten the tone of your stain, either brush more of it out or thin it with mineral spirits before applying.

MIX AND MATCH STAINS. Benjamin Moore's golden oak and colonial maple stains are mixed to create a tint matching new millwork to an old white oak filing cabinet under repair.

My favorite stains are oil-based pigment stains produced by Benjamin Moore and Pratt & Lambert. These stains have finely ground pigments and good solvents. Fine pigments help to eliminate brush marks, and good solvents evaporate quickly and evenly. Cheaper stains use solvents that don't seem to have even-drying characteristics. I have not had success with water-based stains because they raise the grain too much.

To create the tints I need, I combine different stains and add tinting colors (see the sidebar above). But you don't need to buy dozens of different stains. I recommend you get a quart each of Benjamin Moore's walnut and golden oak stains. For tinting, purchase 2-oz. bottles of universal tinting colors (UTCs) in red, yellow, and blue. These are the basic tints used in paints and are available from most paint dealers. With this kit, you can accomplish a lot.

Because I need to match colors of many different woods in my work, I also use maple stains for their yellow cast, cherry stains for their red cast, and a teak stain for its gray-green cast.

On occasion, a good match using premixed colors eludes me, and I resort to mixing my own stain from scratch. I use a clear stain base (I get mine from a local paint dealer) and color it with artist's oils or UTCs. Artist's oils can be used for tinting small batches of stain, but they are expensive.

Just the Topcoat of Stain Gets Dry Brushed

To match the white oak frame to the red oak panels on this job, I applied a base-coat stain to the entire piece, wiped it down in the traditional manner and let it dry. Then a second coat of stain, tinted slightly differently, was applied to the panels. These were dry brushed to match the white oak.

Matching Dissimilar Woods

Every species of wood leans toward certain parts of the color spectrum. In the accompanying chapter, I matched red oak to white oak. I first blended a stain to match the new white oak to the old, but the stain proved to be too red, or warm, for the red oak panels. To remedy this, I added just a few drops of a blue universal tinting color (UTC) to cool the color and make a good match.

If you have a stain that is a bit on the blue, or cool, side but you want more of a mahogany color, simply add some red tint.

It only takes a tiny amount of colorant in some cases to make large changes in tint. I can usually remedy a bit too much colorant by adding a little bit of the other primary colors to balance my mistake. But the more times I have to add a bit of colorant, the harder it will be to duplicate my efforts.

Keep a Variety of Tints on Hand

My color kit consists of a number of artist's oils for small batches of stains, such as for touch-ups, and less-expensive UTCs for large batches.

The artist's oils I have are burnt sienna, raw sienna, burnt umber, raw umber, yellow ochre, permanent blue, alizarin crimson, white, and black.

In UTCs, I keep burnt sienna, raw sienna, burnt umber, raw umber, thalo blue, bulletin red, light yellow, lamp black, and white. Using umbers and siennas is a quick way to get basic browns without the need to mix the primary colors together. Umbers and siennas have a tint built in. With a little experience, you will know which to use as a base.

To get a feel for color matching without mixing a batch of stain, practice mixing colorants on a piece of white tag board. I use toothpicks to get a small amount of tint colorant out of the container, and with a small artist's brush, I mix the colors in varying densities to see what changes occur. Make sure you use a new toothpick for each colorant. Just a little contamination can ruin your mix.

I begin by mixing a base-coat stain and testing it on a piece of scrap from the project. Large differences in grain porosity or wood color—even in the same species of lumber—will affect the results. For the base coat on the filing cabinet, I mixed Benjamin Moore's golden oak and colonial maple stains.

Once I have a good color match, I stain the workpiece (see the top photo on p. 33). When I stained the new parts of the filing cabinet, I was fortunate that the new white oak millwork blended nicely with the old. But the red oak panels were still too warm.

To adjust a stain's color, I add different tints. To cool down the red oak, I added a little blue tint to the base stain and tested it on a sample. This new batch of stain resulted in a perfect color match between the red oak and the white oak, but the tone was still too light. This is where a dry brushing technique comes to the rescue. I brushed the new color stain over the panels. I let the stain set up until it took on a dull sheen. The time will vary from five to 15 minutes, depending on the temperature.

I brushed the stain back and forth with the grain (see the bottom photo on p. 33), using just the tips of the bristles of a clean, dry, soft brush. The weight of the brush does the work. If you press down too hard (see the top photo on p. 36), the stain tends to move around and the brush gets wet. If you use the sides of the bristles or drag the brush at too flat an angle, the stain will smear and leave obvious brush marks.

It's important to keep the brush dry. I use paper towels to wipe the stain off the tips of the bristles after a few passes. If the brush becomes wet with stain, it will only smear the stain, not dry it. Continue to wipe the stain with the brush until the

surface is dry. You know you're done when
the workpiece has a uniform sheen and the
brush no longer picks up stain. The stain
should not show brush marks or any other
obvious signs of a thick topcoat. If the results
are not to your liking, erase the surface
with a rag moistened with mineral spirits.

Overlapping fresh stain over dry-
brushed stain can be a problem. The fresh
stain's solvent will dissolve the built-up
pigment of the dry-brushed stain quickly,
resulting in a poor blend line. Always try to
find natural breaks to stop and start the
brushing, and try to work small areas at a
time. The only exception is a tabletop. Here
I do the entire surface at once. I work fast,
but I never hurry. On a piece that is fairly
complex, such as a chair, I tend to do one
or two parts at a time. Sometimes I'll mask
off completed areas to avoid getting fresh
stain on an already brushed surface.

JUST THE RIGHT TOUCH.
Gently sweep bristles
across workpiece.

Spray on a Protective Finish

A dry-brushed surface needs a protective
coating. Any solvent-based finish will work,
but you must apply it by spraying. A dry-
brushed surface is very delicate because
pigment is floating on top of the wood. If
you try to brush on a finish coat, solvents
will dissolve some of the dry-brushing, and
you'll have a real mess. Handle the piece
carefully before final finishing.

I spray my work with an acrylic lacquer.
I start with one coat of sanding sealer, lightly
sand with 220 grit and then apply two
coats of finish, sanding between them with
220 or 320 grit. If you don't have spray
equipment, you can use aerosol cans of
spray sealer and finish.

KEEP THE BRUSH CLEAN.
Wipe bristles every
few strokes.

ROLAND JOHNSON restores antiques and builds
reproduction furniture and architectural millwork in his
one-man shop in St. Cloud, Minn.

Fuming With Ammonia

Anyone who's spent time mucking out stables, or just walking through a working barn, knows how pungent ammonia fumes are. Those fumes have darkened the beams of many a barn over the centuries. I wouldn't doubt that many farmers put two and two together when they noticed how quickly oak acquired an aged patina.

Around the turn of the century, fuming became popular with many of the furniture makers and manufacturers working in the Arts and Crafts style. So much so that when most people think of Stickley, Limbert, or Roycroft furniture, fumed white oak is what they see in their mind's eye. Other woods can be fumed, but white oak responds best and most predictably to fuming (see the

BY KEVIN RODEL

FUMING WITH AMMONIA gives white oak that classic golden-brown color. Before it's bccn fumcd, whitc oak is a pale, almost cool, tan.

AQUEOUS AMMONIA IS
POURED INTO A GLASS CON-
TAINER placed at the bottom of
the fuming chamber. Then the
top of the chamber is lowered
quickly onto its base. Protective
gear is essential.

sidebar on the facing page). For a look at
the effects of fuming on other woods, see
the sidebar on p. 41.

Regardless of species, boards that will be
fumed should all come from one tree. Different trees within a species will vary in
their tannin content because of growing
conditions. This will affect how they react
to the ammonia. Because it's difficult to get
boards all from one tree at a regular lumberyard, I buy most of my lumber from specialty
dealers who saw their own.

I began fuming furniture because I'd
become increasingly interested in the Arts
and Crafts movement. I had been making
more furniture in that tradition, and I
wanted it to convey the look and feel of
the originals. The finish seemed like an
important element in the whole equation.
Fuming is not the perfect colorant for
every situation and wood species, but
where it does work, it works very well and
can give a superior finish to stains or dyes.

Stains obscure the surface of the wood
somewhat. Worse yet, on ring-porous woods
like oak, pigments collect in large open pores,

making the rings very dark and overly pronounced. The effect is quite unnatural and
looks to me like thousands of dark specks
sprinkled across the surface. Also, stains are
time-consuming to apply, and I have a
strong aversion to exposing myself to the
volatile fumes of the petroleum-based
products found in most commercial stains.

Aniline dyes do a better job than stains,
but they're also rather labor-intensive and
can be very tricky to apply well. Dyes also
fade over time, especially in direct sunlight.
Fumed wood is colorfast.

The thing I like best about fuming is
that what you see after the process is still
only the wood, just as clearly as before. It's
just darker. That's because the ammonia
reacts with tannins that are naturally present
in the wood, actually changing the color of
the wood, not merely adding a superficial
layer of color. Samples of fumed wood that
I've cut open show a ragged line of darker
wood between $\frac{1}{16}$ in. and $\frac{1}{8}$ in. deep.

Another thing I like about fuming is
that it's virtually foolproof. The first piece
you fume will look great. Unlike stains or
dyes, fuming won't make a piece look

blotchy or cause drips. And there's one other benefit to fuming. While the piece of furniture is being fumed, you can get back to work. The ammonia keeps working while you're taking care of other business.

Handle Ammonia With Care

The first and most important consideration when fuming is safety. Before you even buy the ammonia, make sure you have a properly fitted face-mask respirator with ammonia-filtering cartridges. Other types of cartridges, such as those used for spraying lacquer or other finishes, are not designed to filter ammonia fumes and will not offer protection. Ammonia cartridges are inexpensive and available at any fire or safety equipment store. Look in the yellow pages for the one nearest you.

Eye protection is essential. I use swimming goggles, which fit tightly around the eyes. The purpose of the goggles is to protect the eyes from fumes, not just accidental splashes. Rubber or plastic gloves are also necessary. Read the precautions on the side of the ammonia bottle, too.

Finally, if you're trying this for the first time and you work in a basement shop, wait until the weather is nice and do the fuming outside. After you become comfortable with the procedure, you can consider doing it indoors.

The reason for all the precautions when fuming is that ammonia used for fuming wood is not common household ammonia. It is a strong aqueous solution that has between 26% and 30% ammonium hydroxide. Household ammonia has less than 5%.

You'll want to buy the ammonia locally and pick it up yourself. Because it is considered a hazardous substance, shipping charges are high (more than the cost of the ammonia). This industrial-strength ammonia is used in machines that reproduce blueprints and surveys, so you can usually find it at business supply, blueprint supply or surveyor supply stores (look in the yellow pages for a supplier). It's sold by the gallon. Here in Maine, it costs between $6 and $10*. And 1 gal. fumes a lot of furniture.

Bringing Ammonia and Wood Together

With safety equipment and ammonia in hand, you're almost ready to fume. All you need now is some kind of fuming chamber—the more airtight the better. The most versatile and efficient chamber construction seems to be a heavy-gauge (3 mil or greater) plastic wrap stapled to a simple softwood frame that's held together with drywall screws (see the left photo on p. 38). This type of chamber is lightweight, can be made to just about any size, and can be bro-

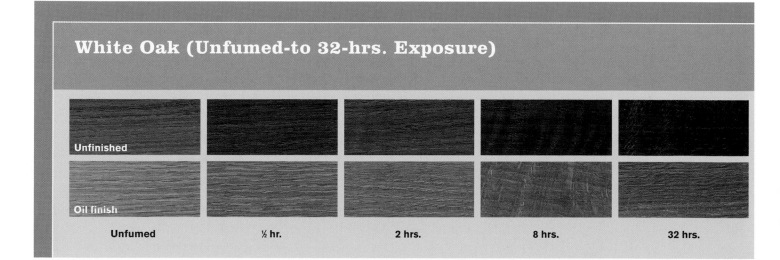

White Oak (Unfumed-to 32-hrs. Exposure)

Unfinished

Oil finish

| Unfumed | ½ hr. | 2 hrs. | 8 hrs. | 32 hrs. |

Unlike stains or dyes, fuming won't make a piece look blotchy or cause drips.

ken down into flat panels for storage. If a fairly large chamber is needed, one side panel can be used as a detachable doorway. Use spring clamps or hand screws to attach the door panel and felt weather stripping as a gasket to seal the chamber.

Small chambers can be placed over the items being fumed, as in the right photo on p. 38. If you're fuming outdoors, be sure to weight or tie down this kind of chamber. They're very light and blow over easily.

I've used many other types of fuming chambers as well—everything from large plastic trash cans (perfect for small items) to a rented moving van. The van allowed me to fume an entire bedroom set at one time for a reasonable cost. The ammonia did no harm to the van, and by the time I returned it the morning after fuming, there was little if any residual smell. And because every piece was exposed to the ammonia for the same amount of time, I was able to achieve a precise color match.

Prepare a piece of furniture to be fumed the same way you would for staining or finishing. Scrape or sand until the surface is smooth, and remove any hardware. Place the piece of furniture in the chamber so that no part that will be visible is touching anything. If the ammonia vapors can't circulate, they won't be able to react with the tannins in the wood. As a result, that spot will not darken like the rest of the piece.

Never let the furniture come into direct contact with the aqueous ammonia because it is very corrosive. I use glass pie plates to hold the ammonia. They're relatively inexpensive, clean up completely, and can be used over and over again. They also present a large surface area to the air so the ammonia evaporates readily.

I fill a plate about half full and place it on the floor of the chamber (see the left

photo on p. 38). The plate should be filled quickly but carefully. If you're fuming a particularly large piece or more than one piece, you may want to use two or three pie plates. Attach the door to the chamber, or lower the chamber onto its base. With the fumes confined to the chamber, you can remove your mask and goggles. Note the time so you can keep track of the exposure.

Test Pieces Determine Color

The length of time a given piece will need to be fumed depends on the volume of the chamber, the amount of ammonia used, the species of wood being fumed, and the depth of color you're looking for. Knowing when to remove a piece is largely a matter of personal experience. You can hedge your bets, though.

The best way to know when you have achieved the desired amount of fuming is to use test pieces. I always place three or four pieces of scrap, preferably cutoffs from the same project, on the floor of the chamber. When I think enough time has gone by, I don mask and goggles, quickly open the chamber, remove one of the scrap pieces, and reseal the chamber.

When it first comes out of the chamber, the wood will have a gray, almost weathered, look. Don't be alarmed; this is normal. To see an approximation of what the finished piece will look like, I apply a coat of finish. As soon as the finish goes on, the real color imparted by the fuming appears instantly, almost magically. If I want the piece darker, I'll continue checking the color of the scrap boards at regular intervals until I'm happy with the result.

If, after eight hours in the chamber, a piece is still lighter than you'd like, you should replace the ammonia. I put on my mask, goggles and gloves, open the chamber, and dump the old ammonia into a bucket of water. I add fresh ammonia to the pie plate, reseal the chamber, and leave the bucket of diluted ammonia outside for a

Fuming Common Furniture Woods

The practice of fuming wood to enhance its color is most often associated with white oak. The oaks in general are high in tannin and fume well, though red oak tends to turn greenish rather than deep brown like white oak. Other species contain varying amounts of tannins and can be fumed, but the effects are generally not as pronounced as with white oak. I was curious about the effects of fuming on other furniture woods, so I fumed a number of them for four hours.

I'd heard that nontannic woods could be fumed if a solution of tannic acid was applied to the surface of the wood first, so I tried that as well. Tannic acid is sold as a powder that you add to water. I added tannic acid to a pint of water until the solution was saturated, applied the solution with a foam brush and then let the samples dry overnight before fuming. Here are the results.

	Unfumed	Fumed	Tannic acid, fumed
Maple — No finish / Oil			
Birch — No finish / Oil			
Cherry — No finish / Oil			
Butternut — No finish / Oil			

day. Then I pour it around the trees in our orchard or on the compost heap.

Once you've decided the wood is dark enough, remove it from the chamber, and let the piece of furniture off-gas for eight to 12 hours. I try to plan my fuming sessions so that the piece comes out of the chamber at the end of the work day. By morning, there's little residual smell.

At this point, you can apply your finish. Oil, varnish, shellac—any finish will work. There's no problem with compatibility between a piece of furniture that's been fumed and the topcoat. At the same time, fuming doesn't protect the surface of a piece in any way, so build up your finish as you would normally.

My preferred finish has always been boiled linseed oil. (I use Tried and True brand because it builds quickly and contains no metal driers). Three or four coats over fumed oak impart a subtle amber overtone that's in keeping with the look of Arts and Crafts furniture.

KEVIN RODEL designs and builds furniture with his wife, Susan Mack, in Pownal, Maine. They have been building furniture, primarily in the Arts and Crafts tradition, for over 17 years.

Please note that price estimates are from 1997.

How to Match a Finish

BY JEFF JEWITT

Sooner or later, most woodworkers will likely face the challenge posed by a client or a spouse: "Well, I know it's pretty wood and all, but can you make it match the rest of the furniture?" The first time I heard those words my heart sank. I had made two matching nightstands for my wife using the most stunning figured ash I'd ever seen. The last thing I wanted to do was stain them, but I had to admit that pearly white wood didn't exactly fit in with our decorating scheme.

Many factory finishing operations involve specialized stains (such as sap stains, equalizing stains, and pad stains) applied to the furniture in as many as six separate coloring steps. But it doesn't have to be that complicated. If you understand how stains work on wood and apply some basic color principles, the job can go a lot smoother. You don't need dozens of different stain colors. Armed with a few dyes and pigment stains in wood-tone colors—plus red, yellow, green, and black—you should be able to match just about anything by following a systematic process of staining, glazing, and clear coating.

Step 1: Establish a Consistent Undertone

A DYE STAIN FOR THE UNDERTONE. Start with a light-colored dye stain to even out different colors in the wood. If you use water-based dye stain, this step also raises the grain.

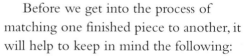

Before we get into the process of matching one finished piece to another, it will help to keep in mind the following:

• Matching a finish requires the correct lighting conditions. Incandescent and some fluorescent lighting will distort the color. It's best to work in diffused natural daylight or under full-spectrum, color-corrected fluorescent lights.

• Work from light to dark gradually. You can always darken a color, but it's very difficult to lighten wood tones under a transparent finish that are already too dark.

• It's easiest to match colors when the finish has a high-gloss sheen. Most colors shift slightly when the finish over them is satin or flat. If the sample you want to match does not have a glossy sheen, wet the surface with some mineral spirits to simulate the effect of gloss.

You Can Build Color in Different Ways

Wood stains can be grouped into two distinct types—dyes and pigments. Manufacturers sometimes mix the two together, but I find it easier to work with one at a time when matching color.

Pigment stains use an inert, finely ground colored powder as the colorant. This powder is suspended in a mixture of resin and thinner. When applied to wood and wiped, the small pigment particles lodge in the surface texture of the wood. When the thinner evaporates, the resin dries and binds the color in place. Soft woods with a spongy texture (such as pine and poplar) have plenty of minute cavities for the pigment to lodge in, so it's possible to make the wood very dark. Hard, dense woods (such as cherry and maple) have

Step 2: Adjust the Color With a Darker Stain

A SECOND, DARKER COLOR OF STAIN SHOULD GET YOU CLOSE. If possible, add this coat when the first one is still wet: It'll help prevent blotches.

fewer cavities, so pigment stains won't work as well if your goal is a dark color.

Dye stains are colored solutions in which microscopic dye particles are mixed with either water or alcohol. When applied to wood, the color is distributed evenly and deeply, so you can stain all types of wood more effectively. The result is a more transparent color than what you get with pigment stains, because dyes don't muddy the surface. And because dyes penetrate deeper and contain no binder that would inhibit absorption, it's easy to shift a color that's slightly off the mark by using another dye.

Glazes are just modified pigment stains. Commercial versions are thicker, have a lower binder content, and they're slower drying because they're sometimes manipulated after application to produce special effects. Add mineral spirits to a pigmented gel stain, and you'll get pretty much the same thing as a store-bought glaze.

Step 3: Fine-Tune the Color With a Glaze

LEARN TO MIX YOUR OWN. Store-bought, oil-based glazes can be tinted with concentrated Japan colors to get the exact shade you want.

GLAZE REFINES THE PROCESS. Liberally coat the workpiece with glaze, then wipe it off.

Step 4: Match the Sheen With a Topcoat

TO MATCH A COLOR, ALWAYS APPLY A GLOSS FINISH. After it dries, you can rub out the surface with fine sandpaper or steel wool to achieve the desired sheen, or you can use a satin or flat finish on the last coat.

Paste wood fillers are pigment stains that contain a fine quartz-silica additive to bulk up the pores of open-grained woods to attain a glass-smooth finish. Oil-based versions are easier to apply and control.

Match a Finish in Four Basic Steps

To match a finish, start with the undertone color of the wood (using dye stains). Over that you often need to change the color using a second dye stain or a pigment stain. When the color is close, add a coat of sealer to lock it in. To tweak the color even more, use a paste wood filler (on porous open grain) or a glaze (on tight grain). And finally, you need to match the sheen of the original finish (with a gloss, satin or flat finish). Using the unfinished cherry side table in the photos to illustrate the process, let's go through each step.

Match the undertone first When matching old furniture or woods that change color easily, this step establishes an underlying golden-colored patina, which evens out different colors in lumber and veneer and helps blend sapwood to heartwood. The undertone is the hardest color to see, but it often is the lightest background color in the wood. It's best to use a dye stain and try it first on a stain board (see the sidebar on p. 46). Also, if you're not sure about the color of the undertone, it's safer to go with a color that is a hair lighter.

Adjust the color, and seal it in Adjust the undertone with a second color of stain, if necessary. This step is more often required with tight-grained woods (such as the cherry shown in these photos) and darker colors. On open-grained woods (such as oak or mahogany), the color of the pores has a dramatic impact on the overall color and appearance of the finish. An oil-based paste wood filler or a glaze will vary that visual impact effectively. Before continuing, you can maintain more control in matching a finish if you first lock in the color with a sealer coat of shellac or lacquer.

Tweak the overall color with a glaze
Once the wood has been sealed and the basic color established, you should need to make only small adjustments to the final color. You can sneak up on it by using a glaze of thinned, concentrated colors. They're easy to apply and, if you get the color wrong, easy to wipe off before they set up. Start with a glaze of wood-tone colors and mix in pure Japan colors such as red or green to adjust the final hue. Check the color of the glaze by smearing some on a piece of glass. When you have the color right, check it on a stain board. To darken a color, use dark brown rather than black, which makes the overall color "cooler," or less red. Swab the glaze on liberally, then wipe it off. A glaze should dry overnight before being covered with a topcoat.

Toning is another good way to produce darker color and tonal shifts, but you'll need to do this with a spray gun by mixing pigment stain or dye stain into the finish.

Match the sheen The color will deepen and go to a shade slightly darker once a clear finish has been applied. Avoid using dark or strongly colored finishes (such as exterior varnishes and orange shellacs) because they will change the final color. If you use a varnish or polyurethane with a gloss sheen, you can rub out the finish to any sheen you wish after the topcoats cure. To determine the sheen of an existing finish, place the sample under a fluorescent light. If the reflection of the tube is distinct, the finish is gloss. If it's slightly fuzzy, the sheen is satin; and if the reflection isn't discernible, the finish has a flat sheen. Gloss topcoats deepen the color the most, and satin and flat sheens lighten up the color slightly or add a frosted look.

JEFF JEWITT restores furniture and sells finishing supplies at his shop in Cleveland, Ohio.

A Stain Board To Guide the Way

To help in the finishing process, make a stain board. Take a scrap cutoff from the piece you're working on and divide it into several sections to give yourself some leeway to tinker with colors until you get a match. You can test colors on the stain board before applying them to your project.

It's surprising how few colors I use regularly to match all the finishes my shop has to produce. For a basic color kit, start with an assortment of four dyes in wood tones: a

honey-colored dye for undertones (especially the yellow undertones on antiques), a medium nut-brown color, a reddish-brown cherry color, and a dark brown. Add red, yellow, and green dyes to modify these wood-tone colors. For pigment stains, you should have comparable colors to those mentioned above plus concentrated versions of red, green, black, and white—sold as Japan colors for oil-based finishes and universal tinting colors (UTCs) for oil- and water-based finishes.

A True Oil Finish

BY CHRIS BECKSVOORT

After 30 years of building and finishing furniture, I still turn to an oil finish for almost all of my work. Oil seeps into the wood and leaves a hand-rubbed sheen that film finishes just can't replicate.

Oil finishes are very popular, and I've tried them all: boiled linseed oil from the hardware store, Watco, Waterlox, Velvit, oil and polyurethane mixes, Livos (now Bio Shield), tung oil, and Minwax. But when Tried & True came on the market in the early 1990s, I decided to use it as my primary finish. It has all of the attributes of an oil finish: spot repairability and easy maintenance, ease of application, and quick build of both the finish and the patina. However, what really sealed it for me was the fact that I would no longer be exposing myself and my customers to toxic metal and petroleum driers contained in most other oils. I have no qualms about using Tried & True for baby cribs, children's furniture, or even cutting boards. Never again will I be dipping my bare hands into "boiled" linseed oil.

Believe it or not, the "boiled" linseed oil you get from the hardware store is not boiled at all. It's raw oil with either petroleum

or heavy-metal driers. Many contain volatile organic compounds (VOCs), which cause air pollution. Even so, they never really dry. The raw, unfiltered oils used in most oil finishes should not be applied to cabinet interiors. When opened, one of my 30-year-old cabinets still greets me with the smell of rancid oil. Tung oil is a decent oil finish, but it takes ages to dry, and it tends to turn yellow.

1 Lay it on. The author heats the finish to 120°F in a glue pot, which makes application easier. Wipe it on with a clean cotton rag. A rubber squeegee can be used for large surfaces.

2 Wipe it off. Allow an hour for the finish to be absorbed, then wipe off any excess with a clean cloth.

3 Rub it out. Once the first coat has dried completely, buff it out with #0000 steel wool. Residue from a dry oil finish will be dusty (like the steel wool on the right), not gummy (as it is on the left).

As far as I know, the only real boiled linseed oil on the market is Tried & True Varnish Oil. This filtered, pure linseed oil is light in color, has a pleasant odor and is very thick. Wiping it is a bit like pushing honey, giving the term "hand-rubbed finish" a whole new meaning.

Tried & True was developed by Joe Robeson, a furniture maker in Trumansburg, N.Y. He found an 1850 formula for producing the oil used in coach-makers varnish. Heat causes the oil to polymerize and absorb oxygen when drying, yielding a bright, durable finish. Robeson found the right boiling time and temperature to produce an oil with great film strength and beauty. The Material Safety Data Sheet is almost too good to be true. It contains less than 0.1% of any substances listed as carcinogens by government agencies. Think about that the next time you stick your bare hands into an oil finish containing petroleum distillates or heavy-metal driers.

Tried & True can be applied over bare or stained wood. The directions say the oil and wood should be at least room temperature (70°F). But heating the oil to 120°F in a glue pot makes it penetrate better.

Apply a thin coat, allow it to penetrate for an hour, then wipe with a soft cloth until the surface is completely dry. A clean rag should not drag or pick up any oil. Allow the finish to dry for 24 hours and then rub it with #0000 steel wool or a soft cloth. Because low temperatures and high humidity tend to slow the drying time, I find that three days between coats works better in my Maine shop. But it's easy to tell whether the finish is dry. When buffing with steel wool, if the residue is gummy, allow more drying time. The residue from a thoroughly dry finish is dusty. I only buff with steel wool after the first coat, preferring to rub with a soft cloth after subsequent coats.

Additional coats deepen the shine and increase protection. I apply three coats on beds, cases, and chairs, and five coats on tabletops (both top and bottom, for even moisture transfer). For me, the finishing process takes about two weeks. However, dust in the shop is not a problem. What I initially found most amazing about Tried & True is that it has a faster surface build than any other oil finish I've found. As with any oil finish, oily rags must be disposed of properly: spread to dry, placed in water, or in an approved, sealed metal container.

Tried & True not only builds fast, but it also lasts. I recently visited a customer who had one of the first pieces I finished with Tried & True. Compared to my early pieces finished with Watco or "boiled" linseed oil, the finish was still bright and shiny.

CHRIS BECKSVOORT is a contributing editor to *Fine Woodworking* magazine.

Sources

Tried & True Varnish Oil
is available directly from the company
607-387-9280
www.triedandtrue-woodfinish.com

Garrett Wade
800-221-2942
www.garrettwade.com

Woodcraft Supply Corp.
www.woodcraft.com

Lee Valley
800-871-8158
www.leevalley.com

A Simple Repair Kit

Spot repairability is a real plus in oil finishing. The author has many customers who need to take out a scratch or water ring or need to re-oil their tabletops every couple of years. He supplies them with a maintenance sheet, #0000 steel wool, paper wipes, and a small bottle of oil. No other equipment is required, nor is a degree in chemistry. One of his favorite reasons for using oil is because the natural color, or patina, develops in a matter of months, not years.

A Hand-Rubbed Oil Finish

BY THOMAS E. WISSHACK

Thomas Sheraton, the 18th-century English furniture designer, recommended making a paste of linseed oil and ground brick dust and rubbing it into mahogany with a piece of cork. The result, enhanced by innumerable polishings with beeswax over the years, is the beautiful patina we see on many treasured antiques.

Oil finishes still have much to offer today's craftsman. An oil finish will accentuate the grain, color, and figure of the wood rather than obscure it, as many coats of a surface finish (such as varnish, shellac, or lacquer) are prone to do. Additionally, an oil finish will never chip, peel or develop fisheye or orange peel. And dust contamination is not an issue with oil finishes, making them a good choice for the craftsman without a separate finishing space. If dust lands before the piece is dry, simply wiping it down with a soft, clean cloth takes care of the problem. Finally, because an oil finish penetrates and bonds with the wood, rather than forming a film atop the wood, renewing the finish is as simple as rubbing in some fresh oil.

As simple and beautiful as oil finishes are, however, it would be a mistake to view oil finishing as a quick, easy solution or a cover-up for bad workmanship. On the contrary, there is quite a lot of work involved in preparing a surface for an oil

finish, and an oil finish will magnify any imperfections in the wood. Also, an oil finish is only moderately resistant to water and alcohol, so it may not be the best choice for a dining room or kitchen table, but for a piece of furniture subject to less spillage and daily wear, it may be ideal. For many craftsmen, the beautiful, rich patina that an oil finish develops over time far outweighs the care needed to maintain it. In this chapter, I'll discuss preparing for and finishing new furniture as well as rejuvenating previously oil-finished pieces.

Surface Preparation

Someone once said that you could put used motor oil on a perfectly prepared wood surface and it would look good. As shocking as that may sound, the statement points out a fundamental truth: An oil finish is only as good as the surface to which it's applied. You may be able to get by with a less than perfectly prepared wood surface if you plan to varnish or lacquer because these finishes form a relatively thick coating. But with an oil finish, any flaws in the unfinished surface will only become more evident when oiled, so you need to take extra care preparing the surface.

Some craftsmen prefer a handplaned or scraped surface to one that has been sanded a great deal. A surface finished by a cutting

50

tool rather than sandpaper possesses a different tactile quality and will respond quite well to an oil finish. Most of us, however, find it necessary to sand at least a bit; how fine a grit you stop at is largely a matter of personal taste. A surface that has been sanded to 1,000 grit will respond as well to an oil finish as one that has been handplaned only, but the characters of their surfaces will differ.

After planing or scraping to remove any mill marks or other imperfections from the wood's surface, you should raise the grain with a sponge or rag soaked in hot water. This will make any unseen flaws in the surface evident, so you can scrape or sand them out. It will also make your project easier to repair if it comes into contact with water after it's finished.

I usually begin sanding with 220-grit wet/dry sandpaper on an orbital sander or hand-held sanding block. I follow up with 320-, 400- and 600-grit paper, always sanding in long, straight strokes with the grain. A pine block faced with sheet cork (available from art supply stores) will keep you from creating valleys as you would if you

held the sandpaper in your hand; this is more important with the coarser grits because of their greater cutting effect. By the time you finish with the 400 grit, you'll start to see the wood grain and color come into focus. With the 600 grit, you're actually burnishing the surface. You may wish to use intermediate grits, or follow the 600 grit with finer automotive sandpapers, but I find the above routine generally sufficient.

After attending to all flat surfaces, I take a piece of worn 600-grit paper and gently round any sharp edges and corners. This will prevent finishing rags from catching and will also give the piece of furniture a slightly used or worn look. If you wish to retain a more open-pored look, or would like handplaning marks to be evident in the finished piece, skip straight from plane to 600- or 1,000-grit paper to polish the surface quite beautifully without filling all the pores (see the photo above).

It's important either to vacuum or to clean the surface thoroughly with compressed air after each successive grade of sandpaper to avoid scratching the surface

ACHIEVING AN OPEN-PORED LOOK is as simple as eliminating all the intermediary sanding and jumping straight from plane or scraper to 600- or 1,000-grit sandpaper. More open-pored woods, such as the wenge in this tabletop, lend themselves better to this treatment than do cherry or maple.

THE HUE OF SUN-BLEACHED WALNUT **suited the author, but the tabletop needed work. Using mineral oil and rotten-stone, he rubbed out numerous minor scratches and scuffs, as well as gave the surface a new shimmer, without changing the color of the wood.**

with particles left over from the previous, coarser grit. I also check the surface with a strong light between each sanding and again when I think I'm done. This will often reveal minor flaws I might otherwise have missed. The wood's surface, ready for oil, should have a sheen and be glass-smooth even before any finish is applied.

I like to let a piece of furniture sit for several weeks after preparing its surface and before I apply any oil. This time allows the surface to oxidize somewhat, giving it a head start on the rich color it will acquire with age. Cherry, for example, will look rather greasy and anemic and may have an unpleasant orangey tone if finished with oil right away. By letting the wood mature

prior to finishing—even for just a couple of weeks—a richer tone results and the patina will build up more quickly. Not all woods respond to this waiting period, and not all craftsmen can afford to wait or are willing to do so. For me, the results are well worth it, and because I normally have several projects going at once, time isn't a problem.

Repairs and Rejuvenation

An oil finish needs to be maintained. I'll refurbish one of my own pieces every couple of years, or sooner if it's damaged. To rejuvenate a surface that is intact (no scratches, water marks, or abrasions), I simply rub my homemade oil finish into the surface for a couple of minutes and then remove all traces of oil with a dry rag. Finally, I rub the surface with another dry, clean rag until the surface has a satiny sheen.

If the surface is scratched or otherwise blemished, it's usually possible to remove the blemish by rubbing it out with a pad of 0000 steel wool soaked in the oil finish. Sprinkling a little rottenstone (a gray, abrasive powder much finer than pumice) onto the wood surface while rubbing will restore its original sheen. If you're removing a blemish from one area, in order to keep the same color and sheen over the whole piece, it's important that you not forget to rub the whole piece out. With each rubdown, the wood gets more beautiful and begins to form a patina. A table I made about ten years ago has had its top rubbed down about six times and is quite striking in appearance.

If a blemish doesn't respond to rubbing out with the steel wool, you may need to use wet/dry sandpaper with the oil solution. Although it depends on how deep the scratch is, as a rule, I don't use anything coarser than 320 grit for repairs. I use a sanding block (to prevent my fingers from digging into the wood) and follow the grain of the wood. Once I've removed the blemish, I work my way through the

Homemade Linseed-Oil Mixture Rubs in Best

Although there are a host of commercially available premixed oil finishes, I prefer to make my own. Call it part nostalgia, but it's the best oil finish I've used. I use this finish only on new furniture. If you're asked to restore an antique, you should seek the advice and expertise of a conservator before proceeding. Although eminently repairable, an oil finish is not removable save by sanding to bare wood.

I mix three parts boiled linseed oil (it must be boiled) to one part turpentine or high-quality mineral spirits and add a few drops of Japan drier (generally available through commercial paint supply stores)—about two percent by volume. For the first coat, I warm the mixture in a double boiler or electric glue pot, being extremely careful to avoid spilling any. I work a liberal amount onto one surface at a time using a natural bristle brush. Then I let the oil sit and soak into the wood for about 30 minutes. Next, I sprinkle the wood surface with a small amount of rottenstone and rub with burlap until a paste develops. I continue rubbing into the wood's surface for several minutes (see the photos at right). Then I wipe all traces of oil and rottenstone off of the piece, using clean, dry rags. Remember that rags saturated with linseed oil are extremely flammable: Submerge them in water immediately after use, or spread them flat outdoors to dry, and then be sure to put them in a closed garbage can outdoors at the end of the day.

I try to let the first coat dry in a well-ventilated, relatively warm area for about two weeks. If any oil beads appear on the surface during this time (they'll usually show up in the first couple of days), I wipe them off with a clean piece of terry-cloth towel. I apply the second coat more sparingly with a soft cotton cloth. After letting the oil soak in for about 15 minutes, I wipe off any oil remaining. I wipe until the rags come off the surface clean and dry and then give all surfaces a brisk rub. Two weeks later, I apply the third coat in the same fashion. If I'm going to apply a fourth or fifth coat, I'll wait another couple of weeks.

The drying time of this finish will vary tremendously depending on atmospheric conditions. The longer you

BURLAP, ROTTENSTONE AND THE AUTHOR'S HOMEMADE LINSEED-OIL MIXTURE combine for a finish that's second to none. Although the paste formed by the rottenstone and oil mixture looks as though it would darken the wood, as long as there are no cracks, the paste will all come off.

can wait the better. It's possible to add more Japan drier to the mixture to ensure drying, but the actual curing of an oil finish takes months and cannot be hastened chemically. Applying too many coats of oil in a short amount of time results in a greasy, slightly transparent tone. It's best to wait until the finish has begun to cure and form the beginnings of a patina before passing the piece on to a customer or gallery.

An oil finish is only as good as the surface to which it's applied.

various grades of sandpaper until I have a perfect surface again, and I finish up with 0000 steel wool and rottenstone. I'm very careful not to sand too deeply because this would expose the underlying (nonoxidized) wood color, necessitating a much more extensive repair. Using the finest grade of sandpaper you can get by with will generally keep you out of trouble.

If you need to repair a piece of furniture but don't want to darken it, rub the piece down with mineral oil instead of a finishing oil. I have a walnut writing table that the sun had started to fade. I liked its color and wanted to retain it, but the tabletop needed some attention. Using the mineral oil just as I've used the homemade finish on other pieces (with a pad of fine steel wool and some rottenstone), I was able to repair the table without changing its color.

Choosing and Applying Oil

As I've tried to stress already, the kind of oil you use isn't nearly as important as the preparation prior to the actual finishing. I generally use a homemade oil finish (see the sidebar on p. 53), but there are also a host of commercially available oil finishes. Danish oil finishes are among the most popular because they're simple to apply and the results are predictably successful.

Second in popularity to Danish oil finishes are tung oil finishes. The working properties of these finishes are similar to the Danish oil finishes, although tung oil generally cures faster and offers a bit more protection than most of the Danish oil products. (Keep in mind, however, that there is tremendous variability in formulation, drying time, and working properties from one manufacturer to another. I've used tung oil finishes that have gone on like Mazola and stayed that way and others that started to tack up almost immediately upon

application.) I find tung oil finishes too shiny, and in some cases, streaky for my tastes, especially with more than two coats, but a final rubdown with fine steel wool will generally both even out the finish and tone the gloss down to a satiny sheen.

My application procedure is similar for Danish oil and tung oil finishes. I brush on a first coat—liberally—and allow it to soak into the wood—about 10-15 minutes for Danish oil finishes but only 2-3 minutes for the tung oil finishes. Then I wipe up all oil remaining on the surface with a clean rag. I let this first coat dry for a few days (for either finish), and then I apply subsequent coats with a rag, wiping in a circular motion. Again, I eliminate all traces of oil remaining on the surface, using a clean, dry rag. Although there's no definite rule on how many coats you should apply, I usually give my pieces three to five coats. It's important to wait as long as possible between coats to avoid the greasy, hurried look that is characteristic of so many oil finishes.

Something to keep in mind, particularly with the more heavy-bodied oil finishes such as the tung oil finishes (although it's true to some degree with all oil finishes), is that the more coats you apply the more you lose the open-pored look. To retain this look on some of my contemporary pieces, I've applied only one coat of oil, and then followed that up a couple of weeks later with a coat of quality paste wax.

In instances where I want to finish a piece with oil, but a greater level of protection is required, I use Formby's Low Gloss Tung Oil Finish. The combination of tung oil and alkyd resins provides considerably more protection than most oil finishes, and the Formby's finish dries quickly and reliably.

THOMAS E. WISSHACK makes and restores fine furniture and is a wood-finishing consultant in Galesburg, Ill.

An Easy, Durable Finish

BY LON SCHLEINING

I wasn't asking for much: I wanted a finish with a rich, hand-rubbed luster, neither too glossy nor too dull, that illuminates rather than hides the grain—one that would offer real protection from moisture and sunlight and yet still feel like wood, not plastic. I also wanted a finish I could apply quickly and easily, and something I could use right out of the can. And it would be awfully nice if it smelled good. That isn't too much to ask of a finish, is it?

The answer turned out to be rather simple: high-gloss spar varnish, turpentine, wet-or-dry sandpaper in various grits, a few rags and a bit of elbow grease. Simply rubbing plain gloss varnish into the raw wood provided the protection, sheen, feel, and ease of application I was looking for.

Start With a Well-Prepared Surface

The key is to scrape, plane, or sand each of the pieces of your project before you assemble it. Even if you have to touch up the sanding after final assembly, this step will save lots of time.

During the building process I sand by machine (belt sander, 120 grit), then sand by hand with a wood sanding block padded

The key is to scrape, plane, or sand each of the pieces of your project before you assemble it.

with felt. The sanding sequence will depend, in part, on the type of wood. On hard maple, for example, use 100 grit, then 120, 150 and finally 220 grit. With mahogany and its much more open grain, stop dry-sanding at 150 grit. Be sure to change sandpaper frequently.

Make sure the surface is clean by using a vacuum to pull out the sanding grit from the pores of the wood. Don't worry if the surface is less smooth than what you normally shoot for. The sanding doesn't stop when the finishing begins. I wet-sand with finer and finer grits during the application of the finish itself.

Materials Are Easy to Obtain

The heart of my finish is a high-gloss spar varnish, which has several advantages: Unlike plain oils, it hardens overnight; it's readily available; and it has much greater clarity than semigloss or satin finishes, whose additives not only dull the finish but also cloud the grain. Spar varnish also contains ultraviolet protection that will help keep the wood from fading or yellowing. I've used this varnish for years on boats, protecting the wood from salt water and abuse, so I know it provides the tough tabletop film I'm looking for. As an added bonus, this finish is quite easy to renew by scuff-sanding with 220-grit paper and simply wiping on an additional coat of varnish if the surface ever needs it. In addition, this finishing method will also work with other types of varnish, urethanes, and even some finishing oils.

Though it's counterintuitive, gloss varnish does not produce a glossy surface when it's rubbed on. Because you're wiping off any excess varnish, not letting it stand on the surface, it doesn't get a chance to build up to its normal gloss.

To thin the varnish for the initial coat, I like to use natural turpentine instead of

paint thinner, simply because it smells good. As a general rule, thin a finish with whatever the label suggests for cleanup.

You will need a few sheets of 220-, 320-, 400-, and 600-grit wet-or-dry sandpaper for sanding in the varnish. For dry-sanding between coats, use open-coat, self-lubricating 320-grit paper. A box of soft cotton rags from the paint store ensures that you won't run out of clean rags just when you need one. Lastly, disposable gloves are essential. Not only will they protect your skin from solvents, but they also make the job a lot less messy.

Application Is Straightforward

Before starting, spread out a plastic sheet to contain drips and spills. This is also a good time to change into an old shirt and pants. (I might even follow my own advice about this one of these days.) Pour a small amount of varnish into a container using a piece of nylon panty hose as a strainer. Thin with one part turpentine to about three parts varnish. The first coat saturates the wood more effectively if it is thinned down a bit.

Wearing gloves, quickly flood the entire surface on all sides until it's completely coated, adding more varnish as needed. It's important to cover the piece completely, not in sections. Working on a small area at a time may leave a line where different areas of finish overlap.

Sand the wet varnish into the wood using 220-grit wet-or-dry paper. Sand with the grain until you produce a slurry. This helps fill the pores of open-grained woods, such as mahogany or oak, and the color match is perfect. While the varnish is still wet, wipe with a soft cotton rag to remove any varnish that has not soaked into the wood. When removing the excess varnish, there's a point at which the varnish gets quite sticky and difficult to wipe. Working on something like a large tabletop might require a helper. Rub across the grain to

First Coat: Thinned Varnish

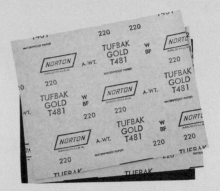

Three Parts Varnish   **One Part Thinner**   **220-Grit Wet-or-Dry Paper**

APPLY THE FINISH LIBERALLY. It is important to coat the whole surface as quickly as possible to avoid creating lines where the finish overlaps. The author uses his gloved hands to spread the thinned varnish over the surface before sanding it in with 220-grit wet-or-dry paper.

GRAIN FILLER WITH A PERFECT COLOR MATCH. Sanding the varnish with the grain creates a slurry that fills the pores of open-grained wood.

avoid pulling the slurry out of the wood pores. Be sure to spread out the oil-soaked rags to dry before disposing of them, to avoid the danger of the rags spontaneously igniting.

Buff with a fresh cloth until the surface is slick and smooth. Polish the piece every half-hour or so to make sure no wet spots emerge on the surface. Joints, such as on the breadboard ends of a tabletop, will absorb excess varnish, which will gradually seep

out after the rest of the surface has dried. To avoid this, I blast the joint with compressed air, forcing the surplus varnish out of the gap.

Let the piece sit at room temperature overnight. You can carry on working in the shop because it doesn't matter if dust lands on the piece, but it is a good idea to ensure adequate ventilation to avoid a concentration of fumes. The next morning the surface should feel smooth and dry. Lightly dry-sand it with 320-grit nonloading, or

NO PLACE FOR SURPLUS VARNISH TO HIDE. No matter how much you wipe, varnish has a habit of oozing out of joints after you have done your final buffing, creating sticky and glossy areas. Remove surplus varnish using compressed air, and wipe the area clean.

SAND ON AND WIPE OFF. Before the varnish becomes tacky, wipe off the surplus using clean cotton rags. Keep changing the rags until no more finish can be removed and the surface can be buffed smooth.

stearated, paper. Use a felt-padded block, and sand with the grain. Clean the surface with a vacuum or compressed air. Apply a flood coat of unthinned varnish and use 320-grit wet-or-dry paper to sand the varnish into the surface. Wipe and buff the excess varnish as before.

Repeat this process each day; wet-sanding with finer and finer grits until you have at least three coats. Additional coats will produce slightly more luster. Some folks like to wax the surface when it's dry, but I prefer to leave it unwaxed, because it's easier to

recoat should the surface become damaged over time.

I haven't yet been tempted to throw away either my spray guns or my badger-hair brushes, but after using this finishing process on several projects, I can't remember the last time I used those tools. This simple technique meets all of my criteria for an ideal finish and produces very consistent results, all without a large investment in equipment.

LON SCHLEINING, a woodworker in Signal Hill, Calif., is the author of *The Workbench*.

Additional Coats: Unthinned Varnish

Unthinned Varnish

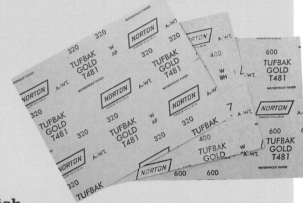

Finer-Grit Paper

SCUFF-SAND THE SURFACE THE FOLLOW-ING DAY. Between coats, lightly sand the surface using 320-grit nonloading, or stearated, paper under a padded block. Always sand with the grain.

BUILD THE FINISH. Apply subsequent coats the same way as the first coat. Rub in each coat with a higher grit of wet-or-dry paper. The last coat is rubbed in with 600-grit paper to create a very smooth surface.

A FINAL BUFFING. After the final coat has dried, the surface will be silky smooth with the pores filled. Rub the surface briskly with a clean cotton rag.

Choosing and Using Brushes

BY DAVID SORG

Brushing on a finish involves considerably less expense, space, and even danger than spraying. The results can be as perfect as any sprayed finish, requiring only a little more time. I earn an added bonus when using a brush instead of a spray gun. Holding the brush, dipping it into the finish and then letting it glide onto the wood brings my project to life and provides me with a unique satisfaction. Choosing the right brush can save you hours in application speed and ease of use. Proper technique will help you avoid or minimize mistakes and brush marks.

I have two rules when it comes to buying a finishing brush. First, don't buy anything with a plastic handle. I've never seen a high-quality brush that didn't have a wooden handle. Use the plastic-handled ones for staining wood or painting your shed.

The second rule of thumb is to buy the best brush you can afford. To put things in perspective, for less than the cost of a good router you can buy a set of top-of-the-line brushes that will meet all of your finishing needs. No wonder my woodworking friends are jealous.

Brushes can be divided into four broad categories: natural bristle, synthetic bristle, artist's brushes, and nonbrushes, such as foam wedges and pads. I will guide you through each group and suggest which brushes will match your preferred type of finish and the piece you are finishing.

Natural Bristles Are the Prima Donnas of Brushes

Natural-bristle brushes are considered the best choice for lacquer, shellac, and oil-based finishes. These brushes can hold more finish than their synthetic alternatives, an important issue for flowing shellac or lacquer. With these finishes you must maintain a wet edge, and the fewer the trips to recharge the brush, the better. Natural-bristle brushes seem to transmit a better feel for even-finish distribution. I can more easily sense the degree of slickness or drag beneath the natural bristles, especially when tipping off to achieve a smooth surface. But I'd be the first to admit that it may just be the fact that I've been using natural bristles for nearly 20 years.

The disadvantages of natural bristles include a faster rate of wear and breakage of the bristles (which are a pain to pick out of your finish coat, especially if it's fast-drying lacquer or shellac), and they are harder to clean than synthetics.

Synthetic Brushes Are Getting Better

A few years ago you would have used a synthetic brush only with a water-based finish. But synthetic brushes have come a long way since the early days of blunt-ended nylon bristles. Tynex and Chinex are among the brand names you'll see on better full-sized brushes. The latest addition from Purdy is Syntox. When applying alkyd varnish, a Syntox brush leaves as few brush marks as a natural-bristle brush does, and it works as well with water-based finishes as any other brush I've tried.

For Smaller Areas, Choose an Artist's Brush

Artist's brushes are made from a variety of natural and synthetic materials. For $3 to $6* you can get ⅛-in. and ¼-in. brushes made from synthetic Taklon that are useful for touch-ups. A 1-in. brush is handy for small projects, such as drawers, or thin edges. The most useful artist's brush for applying shellac or solvent varnishes is the 1½-in. or 2-in. wash brush. Offered by companies such as Winsor & Newton, a wash brush is a very soft blend of Taklon and natural bristles (or pure Taklon). It allows you to float or "wash" on thinned-down finishes with virtually no brush marks.

Use Foam Pads and Wedges for Stains and First Coats

Last, and generally least, are the nonbrushes—foam wedges and pads that come on the end of a handle. These are cheap and useful for staining and applying first coats of most clear finishes where much of the product will be wiped or sanded off. But be cautious using them with lacquers, which may melt the foam. Also, the alcohol in shellac may dissolve the glue that attaches the foam to the handle.

Because material from these pads is squeezed out by applying more pressure, achieving an even finish is difficult. Particularly with pieces that have lots of edges, moldings, or carvings, you're more likely to get runs as you try to make the pad conform to the contours of the piece.

Don't Be in a Rush to Brush

Much as the steering wheel of a sports car transmits the feel of the road, with experience you'll be able to sense when the brush is flowing material onto the surface at the

Choosing the right brush can save you hours in application speed and ease of use.

proper rate. You'll feel the subtle differences between areas that are puddled too thickly and the extra drag from spots that have been skipped entirely.

Developing this feel takes practice. Make up a sample in the same wood and in some of the same profiles that appear in your project. Aside from helping you decide which brush feels right for the job, the sample will help you determine a finishing schedule; the correct stain color; how many coats to apply; whether thinning is necessary; when to sand and with what paper; and how the final finish will feel and look.

The easiest way to finish a project is to take it apart into its smallest components. It is also important to determine what order you will brush the various surfaces of your project. Dovetailed drawer fronts, in particular, are much easier to finish cleanly when not yet attached to their (usually) unstained and/or unfinished sides.

Remove all hardware or carefully mask any that must remain. In general, work from the top down, from the inside out, from a panel to its stiles and rails. The goal is to reduce the number of wet edges that you must try to keep so that the finish can integrate or melt into itself without leaving brush marks or ridges. Try to break down everything to a series of small panels, strips of moldings, or blocks of carvings.

Getting the Brush Wet

After straining the finish into another container and adjusting its viscosity, if necessary, load the brush with the finish material. It's important to pay attention to how much finish you are placing into each brush load. Too much material, and you'll drip finish across the surface as you head for the area to be worked, or it will puddle the moment you lay the brush on the surface. If you pick up too little, it will

mean more trips to the can and more time for wet edges to set up before the next brush load gets there.

Adjust each brush load for its intended surface; for instance, a flat tabletop takes all you can give it, while a ¾-in.-wide by 12-in.-long drawer edge barely needs the tips of the bristles wetted.

Start each panel at the edge farthest from you. This way, if you drip onto unfinished areas, you'll be able to go right over the drips. If practical, work with the grain.

Takeoffs and Landings on Tabletops

On your first stroke you have two edges—one parallel to the grain and direction of the brush stroke and one perpendicular to the grain and stroke. Land the brush just in from the perpendicular edge and move it about ⅛ in. from the parallel edge until you run out of finish. Don't lean on the brush. Now return to where you started the stroke and brush off the perpendicular edge. The biggest cause of runs and drips is brushing onto an edge, which allows surplus liquid to dribble down the side of your project.

Finally, reverse the direction of the brush and lightly glide it from where the original stroke ended and go off the perpendicular edge. This process is called tipping off and should leave an even amount of finish that is as wide, or slightly wider than, the width of the brush. On a small surface, you may be able to go right off the other perpendicular edge as well. In this case, your tip-off stroke will be more like an airplane touch-and-go landing, coming in lightly an inch or so from one edge and taking off at its opposite edge.

On a larger surface, you have two choices for beginning your next stroke with a recharged brush. Some prefer to bring down the brush just inside the wet area where it began to thin out, then continue on toward the far edge. Others prefer to

Brush Types, Sizes, and Shapes

Natural Natural bristles are still the standard that synthetic ones try to match. Most people associate badger hair with natural bristle, but pure badger-hair brushes are too soft for applying most finishes. The stiffest bristles are hog or Chinese bristle, which come as either white or the slightly stiffer black. Most all-purpose natural-bristle brushes are a blend of hog bristles and either badger or ox hairs. Costing $20 to $30*, natural-bristle brushes are expensive. And because natural-bristle brushes absorb so much water and become limp, they are not a good choice for water-based products.

Synthetic Synthetic bristles used to be confined to water-based finishes that were unsuitable for natural bristles. They have always been cheaper and easier to maintain than their natural counterparts, and as their quality has improved, growing numbers of finishers are switching to them for all types of finishes. Names of some of the better bristles are Chinex, Tynex, and Syntox, but avoid bristles described only as nylon, polyester, or a blend of the two.

Three Sizes to Fit Your Needs A 3-in. brush, a 2½-in. angled sash brush, and a 1½-in. brush with either natural or synthetic bristles cover most finishing requirements in woodworking. An angled sash brush can cover wide surfaces and get into tight spots. In general, always use the largest brush that can fit into the area to be finished. The carrying capacity of the larger brush means fewer trips to the can to reload and makes it easier to maintain a wet edge and avoid overlap streaks.

Oval Brushes for Large Areas If you have a large surface to finish, consider purchasing a brush with an oval-shaped ferrule (the metal band between the handle and the bristles). These brushes can hold a lot of material, allowing large areas to be finished before reloading. However, it's more difficult to obtain a smooth surface using an oval brush.

Artist's Brushes for Small Areas Artist's brushes can fit into tight areas. The 1½-in. wash brush with synthetic Taklon bristles will apply a final coat of thinned shellac or oil-based finish that leaves almost no brush marks. Expect to pay $25 to $55* for these brushes.

Finishing a Tabletop

Load the Brush

STRAIN THE FINISH. After a can has been opened several times, dried finish collects around the lid and bits of skimmed-over finish may be floating inside. Remove all of this debris by passing the finish through a paint strainer.

CLEARLY BETTER. Pouring some finish into an empty container allows you to thin only the finish you'll use. Select a container that the brush easily enters, and adjust the volume to reach halfway up the bristles.

ADJUST THE LOAD. Push the brush gently against the side of the container to strain out the desired amount of finish. Do not scrape the brush against the rim of the container because it can cause bubbles in the liquid.

Start at the Edge

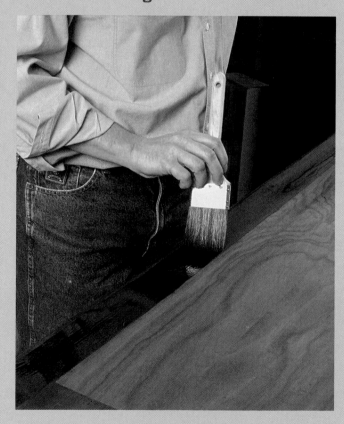

BEGIN JUST INSIDE THE CORNER OF THE TABLE. Continue about ⅛ in. from the edge closest to you. After exhausting the finish, come back and brush off the edge where the stroke began.

THEN PULL OFF THE EDGE. Short strokes with the tip of the brush finish the edge of the table. A curved profile is the hardest edge to finish because of the lack of a clearly defined boundary.

CONTINUE THE FIRST STRIP. Start in the dry area and brush back into the feathered edge before reversing direction and carrying on to the far edge.

Work Across the Top

PREVENT POOLING. With thicker finishes, leave a gap between strokes.

BLEND THE LINES TOGETHER. The tip-off stroke fills the gap, creating a finish of uniform thickness.

LOOK OUT FOR PUDDLES. Occasionally look at your work from a low angle to check that the finish is being applied evenly. Slow-drying finishes can be leveled simply by rebrushing.

begin a few inches into the dry area, brushing toward the feathered edge and into it, then reversing the stroke and carrying it toward the far edge. Which technique you choose will depend partly on how fast you work; for example, with lacquer and shellac you run a risk of pulling out the drying finish if you start inside of it.

Continue your finishing pattern until you reach the far edge—spreading out a brush full of material, then tipping off to merge the stroke with the previous one.

Begin the next stroke by laying down the edge of the brush either immediately next to the first stroke or slightly separated from it. With thin shellacs and lacquers that will melt into each other, I usually lay up the edges to the previous stroke or even overlap them slightly. With thick varnishes, I keep the strokes separated, then blend the edges by tipping off. Water-based varnishes require this blending to be done quickly; oil varnishes give you plenty of time.

Continue until you complete the panel, checking the adjacent edges for any rollover that can be wiped off an otherwise dry surface. If the other surface is wet, it's best to let the drip dry and sand it rather than try to brush it out.

Run-Free Raised Panels

Start with the bevel surrounding the center panel. Beginning the brush stroke right in a corner tends to cause pooling. If anything, interior corners can be starved of finish to yield a crisper look. Start the stroke ⅛ in. away and discharge the brush as you head for the opposite corner. Come back with the nearly dry brush to blend the beginning of the stroke into the first corner.

Brush the flat section of the panel the same way you would a small tabletop: Start the stroke just inside one edge and brush off the far edge. Return to brush off the first edge, and finally tip off the whole strip with a touch-and-go pattern, avoiding brushing onto either edge.

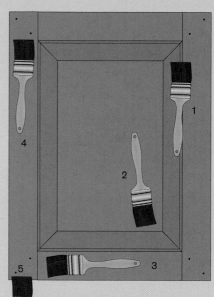

Paint by Numbers

Brush a raised panel in the following order to achieve a flawless finish:

1) Start on the panel bevel, working away from a corner.

2) Treat the panel center like a small tabletop.

3) Brush the rails of the frame.

4) Finish the stiles—brushing off, not onto, either end.

5) With the tip of a barely wet brush, finish the edge last.

1 BEGIN WITH THE BEVEL. Bring down the brush away from a corner to avoid pooling the finish. Brush with the grain whenever possible. Once the stroke has been completed, use the tips of the bristles to push a small amount of finish into the corner.

2 THINK OF THE PANEL AS AN AIRCRAFT CARRIER. Land the brush inside the near edge of the panel and continue the stroke until you "fly off" the far edge.

Then do the strip of molding that surrounds the panel, or the entire rail or stile if there is no decorative edge. If the rails butt into the stiles, brush the rails first, starting and stopping as close to the joint as possible (slightly over the edge onto the stile is better than coming up short of it). For these strokes, you'll want a slightly less loaded brush because you're going to stroke to a line instead of going off an edge, and you don't want to leave a roll of material. With oil-based varnishes you can just stroke right out onto the stile because it will stay wet long enough to be picked

up when you brush the stile. Finally, finish the edges of the whole assembly.

Brushing Narrow Boards

Brushing a board that is wider than the width of your brush but not as wide as two brush widths is tricky. Brush a coat of finish down the middle of the board, stroke out to each of the three remaining edges, then tip off with a couple of strokes parallel to the grain.

If the board is narrower than your brush, turn the brush on an angle to make its effective width the same as the wood. This is where an angled sash brush is often convenient. When you are brushing edges of

4 BRUSH THE STILES AS YOU WOULD A TABLETOP. **Start inside the near end, continuing to the far end, then come back to brush off the near edge.**

3 THE RAILS NEED SPECIAL ATTENTION. **If the rails butt into the stiles, brush the rails first, starting and stopping as close to the joint as possible.**

5 LEAVE THE EDGE UNTIL LAST. **Apply a line of finish using the tip of the brush, then pull it off each edge.**

Sources

Purdy brushes can be viewed at www.purdy-corp.com and are available at most paint stores and home-improvement centers.

Specialized natural- or synthetic-bristle brushes can be purchased at the following web sites: www.finepaints.com and www.homesteadfinishing.com.

boards or doors, hold the brush perpendicular to the surface and use just the tip to lay a bead of finish down the center of the strip from one end to the other. Again, using the tip of the brush, spread the center roll of material to each edge across the grain. Last, do a long, light tip-off stroke following the grain.

Carvings and Latticework

Carvings can be finished in shellac or lacquer by using a small artist's brush. First, coat undercuts and recesses with a lightly loaded brush, then brush the tops and primary surfaces, allowing the edges of the finish to melt together. Additional coats are usually just placed on highlights that can be lightly sanded, if necessary. Surfaces that will be rubbed and polished require more finish.

When brushing oil varnish, apply it more liberally, then pick out any pools with a discharged brush. To even out the coverage in the area, use a dry brush and work in short, vertical motions (called stippling). Water-based finishes can be worked in a similar manner, but in small sections to keep the working area wet.

DAVID SORG is a professional finisher and artist in Denver, Colo.

* Please note price estimates are from 2002.

Making a Case for Varnish

BY FRANK POLLARO

I'd just finished the most complex piece I had ever attempted, the reproduction of a desk by Emile-Jacques Ruhlmann, the greatest of the Art Deco furniture designers. The curvaceous desk, veneered in amboyna burl and shagreen, or stingray skin, had taken me more than 300 hours to complete. The original had been French polished, but I wanted to provide my reproduction with more protection than shellac affords while giving it the same clarity and brilliance.

I asked Frank Klausz, a friend and fellow woodworker, what he recommended, and he suggested that I use varnish. I experimented on scrap boards until I was satisfied with the results. And then I varnished the desk. It was the perfect finish with all the depth, clarity and brilliance I had hoped for.

Now varnish is the standard finish for all my fine work (see the photo on the facing page). I've experimented with a number of varnishes and brushes and refined my technique. Now I can brush on a finish that looks as though it has been sprayed.

Understanding Varnish

A properly applied varnish finish is glass smooth, hard and resistant to most household chemicals, foods, and drinks. It also has a warm, amber glow. That makes it best suited for darker woods, unless you want to add warmth to a light wood, such as maple or ash. Regardless of the choice of wood, a well-polished varnish surface will turn heads.

Varnish must be rubbed out About the only downside to using varnish is that you have to rub out and polish the finish if you want a blemish-free surface. Varnish is oil based, so it takes far longer to dry than lacquer or shellac. Lacquer thinner and denatured alcohol evaporate in minutes, leaving a hard, dry finish behind. Varnish can stay tacky for hours, vulnerable to anything in the air, whether that's dust or a wandering fly. So it's important to apply varnish in as clean an atmosphere as possible.

Depending on the style and function of the piece of furniture I'm finishing, as well as the client's tastes, I may polish it only to a satiny gloss, or I may take it all the way to a high gloss. Either way, though, it's not nearly as time-consuming as a lot of woodworkers think it is. Even a very large dining table won't take more than an afternoon to rub out and polish.

You must sand between coats The other major difference between varnish and lacquer is that you cannot reactivate dried varnish with a fresh coat or with a solvent. With lacquer, every time you apply a new coat of lacquer, you effectively melt it into previous coats, creating what amounts to a single, thick coat. With varnish, you're building up a finish one layer at a time. Each new coat should bond mechanically to the one below it by gripping the scratches in the surface. For this reason, it's absolutely essential to sand between coats until there are no shiny, low spots.

One final detail about the varnish itself. Always use a high-quality product. It will brush on and flow out much better than cheaper stuff. I've settled on Behlen's Rockhard Tabletop varnish (see Sources on p. 70). It's the best varnish I've found, and it dries the hardest, so it rubs out better than any other.

ALWAYS USE A GOOD BRUSH.
Look for a thick, firm brush with fine bristles, like this badger brush.

Sources

Behlen's Rockhard Tabletop varnish:
Garrett Wade
800-221-2942

Woodworker's Supply
800-645-9292

Kremer Pigments
228 Elizabeth St.
New York, N.Y. 10012
212-219-2394

Meguiar's Mirror Glaze #1 Meguiar's at
800-854-8073

A Good Brush is the Key

The single most important thing you can do to achieve a great varnish finish is to start with a good brush. They aren't cheap—expect to spend between $30 and $60* for a 3-in. brush. My first varnish brush was a badger brush from Behlen's (see the photo above), which I still use. It's a good value at $30 or so. But I discovered another brush last year that I like even better. It's made in Germany from the inner ear hair of oxen and is imported by Kremer Pigments (see Sources at left). The brush, listed simply as the Pi72, costs nearly $60*. But it has very fine bristles, which leave virtually no brush marks in the finish surface.

Whichever brush you decide to use should be thick, firm, and made with fine, natural bristles. This will allow the brush to hold a good amount of varnish and distribute it evenly on the surface. A thin, skimpy brush won't hold enough varnish. A limp brush won't move the varnish around, and coarse bristles can leave marks in the finish. If you're going to use varnish, do yourself a favor and buy a good brush.

Brushing It On

The best place to varnish a piece of furniture is in a small, dust-free room with the windows closed. Few of us have that luxury, though. To reduce the number of little dust specks settling on the wet varnish, I often spray a mist of water in the air, on the ceiling and on the floor just before getting started. Try not to get any water on the piece you're about to finish. Don't get too worked up about dust, though, because any small bumps will be sanded off after each coat has dried.

I cut the first coat of varnish 50% with thinner and add a few drops of Behlen's Fish Eye Flo-Out. This is essentially just silicone, but it enhances the flow of the varnish, eliminates the likelihood of fisheyes, and improves the scratch resistance and glossiness of the finish.

Brush technique is important with varnish. The object is to apply a thin, even coat. If you put on too much varnish, it will skin over and the varnish under the skin will never dry. If you use too little varnish, you'll have a hard time moving it around, and it will not flow out. With a little practice, though, the whole process will become second nature.

I find it helpful to let the brush soak in the varnish for a minute or two, so it can absorb some of the finish. Then I apply the first coat, brushing all the way across the table in long, smooth strokes (see the top photo on the facing page). After covering the table with varnish, I quickly brush over the varnish I've just applied, but at 90° to the original direction and with a much lighter touch (see the bottom photo on the facing page). Each coat is applied in the same way. On a piece of furniture with a predominant grain direction, I apply the varnish first across the grain and then brush it with the grain. You have to move quickly because even though the varnish will stay tacky for hours, it will start to set up after

BRUSH ON THE VARNISH IN LONG, SMOOTH STROKES. On a surface with a single or a predominant grain direction (unlike this sunburst veneer pattern), start by applying the finish across the grain. The first coat of varnish should be a 50/50 solution of varnish and solvent.

BRUSH OUT THE VARNISH AT 90° to the direction you laid it on, usually with the grain. Use a light touch. Just skim across the surface without exerting any downward pressure.

just a few minutes. You'll probably see brush marks, or striations, in the surface at first, but after 15 minutes or so, they'll level out.

I let this first coat dry for at least 24 hours and then sand it out with a random-orbit sander and a 220-grit disk. This gives the surface some tooth for the next coat to bind to. After sanding, I wipe down the surface with a tack cloth before applying the next coat.

I brush on the second coat, cut with 25% thinner and then wait another 24 hours for the coat to dry before sanding it. For a tabletop like this one, I'll apply four or five coats, allowing 24 hours between each coat and 72 hours after the last coat before starting to rub out the finish. The third and subsequent coats are full-strength varnish. Four coats are usually enough, but I've applied as many as eight. If you want the surface to be completely smooth and non-porous, keep applying coats until there are no pores showing after you've sanded with the 220-grit paper. Then just one final coat should do it.

Rub Out and Polish the Finish

When you're happy with the last coat and have given it at least 72 hours to dry (a week would be better), it's time to rub out the finish. For a satin finish, I just sand with 600-grit paper and polish with 0000 steel wool lubricated with Behlen's Wool-Lube. Then I rub down the surface with a clean cloth, and I'm done.

RUB OUT NUBS OR BUMPS with 1,200-grit paper wrapped around a wooden block. Water, naphtha, or mineral spirits may be used to lubricate the surface.

USE A RUBBER SQUEEGEE TO CLEAR SLURRY. The 1,200-grit paper works slowly, so keep rubbing and clearing the slurry until all the high spots are gone.

POLISH THE FINISH WITH A POWER BUFFER AND AUTOMOTIVE GLAZE. Once you've sanded out all the nubs and bumps and gotten the surface flat, 10 minutes of power buffing will take the finish to a high-gloss shine.

For a high-gloss finish, I used to wet-sand from 600-grit to 1,000-, 1,200- and, finally, 1,500-grit paper. Now I start and end my sanding with 1,200-grit paper (available at most auto-body supply shops). The advantage of working your way through the grits is that the rubbing out takes less time and the result is likely to be slightly flatter because you're starting with a more aggressive abrasive. The reason I stopped doing it is that I always found myself trying to eliminate a scratch or two from one of the coarser grits that only became apparent after I'd gotten to the 1,500 grit. I'd have to go through the whole routine again, losing any time I had saved.

To take down all the nubs or bumps in the surface of the finish caused by dust or other debris, I wrap the sandpaper around a wooden block (see the top left photo). I've used naphtha, mineral spirits, and water as wetting agents. For this table, I used water with a little Behlen's Wool-Lube in it to make things more slippery. A little rubber squeegee helps to clear away the slurry, so you can check to see if a bump is gone or if you have more sanding to do (see the top right photo on the facing page). The auto-body supply dealer I do business with gives me these squeegees.

After I've sanded out all of the nubs and bumps, I swap the wooden block for a cork block and give the whole table an even sanding, trying to get it as flat as possible. It's important to take down any high spots after each coat. If you let these spots build up, you could sand through one coat into another. This shows up as a visible ring between the two coats, and the only way to fix it is to sand off the whole topcoat and apply it again.

Pay special attention to the edges, where the varnish can build up a little ridge. You can judge how flat the finish is by looking at the reflection of a light on the table. If it looks like it's reflecting off the surface of a wind-swept pond, then you have some more sanding to do. If it's relatively undistorted, you're in good shape.

To complete the gloss finish, I apply Meguiar's Mirror Glaze #1 (an automotive rubbing compound; see Sources on p. 70), buff it out, and wipe it off. It's important to get the surface completely clean because any residue from the #1 compound will scratch the surface when you go to the next finer compound. I follow the Meguiar's #1 with the #3 compound, using a different buffing wheel—again, so the residue from the coarser compound doesn't undo what I'm trying to accomplish (see the bottom photo on the facing page). After buffing with the #3 compound, I wipe off the table with a clean rag. The surface will shine like a mirror.

FRANK POLLARO designs and builds custom furniture in East Orange, N.J.

Please note that price estimates are from 1996.

For Porous Woods, Fill the Grain

On very open-grained woods, such as burls, I collect all of the sawdust from my final dry-sanding (220 grit) in a jar. I mix this sawdust with full-strength varnish (see the top two photos below). I hone a square edge on a 2-in. putty knife and use it to apply this paste to the raw wood in place of the 50% dilution I normally use for the first coat.

I lay this paste down in one direction and spread it perpendicularly. I fill the voids, imperfections and pores (see the bottom photo), being careful not to scratch the surface. After 24 hours, I sand with 220 grit to reveal a glass-smooth surface. Two more full-strength coats of varnish and I'm ready to rub out and polish the finish.

MIX FULL-STRENGTH VARNISH and 220-grit sanding dust until it has the consistency of molasses.

WORK MIXTURE INTO THE GRAIN. Apply it in one direction, and then work it into pores crosswise. Try to create a smooth surface.

Oil-Varnish Mixture Is Durable, Easy to Apply

BY GARRETT HACK

Finishing just isn't my cup of tea. Planning the design and construction details, picking the wood, and carefully laying out the parts to match the wood's color and grain are all exciting. Cutting joints and planing by hand are pure pleasure. But putting on a finish is my least favorite part of building furniture. That may be one reason I've settled on a finish that gives me consistently satisfying results with a minimum of effort.

I first learned about this hybrid finish—a mixture of oil, varnish, and turpentine—at the woodworking school I went to in Boston in the late 1970s. Since then, I've experimented with the ingredients, the proportions, and the method of application. These days, I use this finish on everything from fine furniture and kitchen cabinets to the handles on the tools I use around my farm.

The finish is mixed from either tung oil or boiled linseed oil and varnish, thinned with turpentine. It's easy to apply, doesn't require a special dust-free finish room, and, like any oil finish, it won't obscure the texture and character of the wood. Yet because of the varnish, it offers more protection than oil alone.

The varnish also helps the finish build faster than a straight oil finish, eliminating much of the drudgery of application. Because the proportion of varnish is relatively low, this finish is as easy to repair or renew as an oil finish. And it can be tinted with artist's pigments or oil-based stains to match any wood. There's no need to fill pores on open-grained woods: Sanding the finish creates a slurry of wood dust, oil, and varnish that fills the pores beautifully.

Don't Sweat the Finish Proportions

When mixing this finish, I don't get overly scientific about measurements. The finish is very forgiving, and many proportions will work. Generally, I mix them in approximately equal measures. If I want more protection, I'll add up to 50% more varnish. If it's too thick (and always for the first coat), I'll add more turpentine to get better surface penetration. If I'm going to color the mixture, I add an oil stain or artist's colors, keeping it light initially and darkening it more if need be.

Spar Varnish Is a Favorite

Varnishes have been around for a long time.
Really old-fashioned varnishes are a mixture of plant resins (such as amber), oils, and
a solvent, which is heated and combined in
formulations often kept secret by their
makers. Even the techniques for applying
these varnishes are carefully guarded by the
few who still use them. Some of these varnishes take weeks to cure fully.

Modern varnishes are a combination
of synthetic resins in an oil vehicle. Among
the oils used by finishing manufacturers
are soya, safflower, tung, and linseed. The
proportion of oil to resin in these varnishes
ranges widely, and this affects how long
they take to cure, as well as how tough and
how elastic the cured finish film will be.

A spar varnish has a comparably high oil
content, which takes longer to cure and
leaves a fairly elastic surface that accommo-
dates wood movement. Polyurethane varnishes dry quickly and form a tough,
durable, but less elastic, coating. Also, after
the finish has cured, repairs or additional
coats don't bond well.

INGREDIENTS ARE SIMPLE; PROPORTIONS ARE FORGIVING. **Linseed or tung oil, varnish, and turpentine make up the author's favorite finish. A pigmented oil stain can be added to give the mixture a little color.**

In terms of drying time, toughness, and elasticity, alkyd-resin varnishes fall somewhere between spar varnish and polyurethane. They're not as tough as polyurethane, but they're more elastic, and any coats applied after the varnish has cured still bond well.

I have used all three of these varnishes in my finish with good results, but my favorite is spar. The main reason is color. Spar is the darkest. In combination with linseed oil, which also tends to darken wood, spar varnish significantly affects the color of some woods, like cherry. I happen to like the effect this mixture has.

Right away, cherry and bird's-eye and curly maple look older. But on darker woods like walnut, the color change is barely perceptible. If you want to preserve the light color of a wood like maple or ash, use a polyurethane varnish because it imparts the least color.

Most varnishes also have ultraviolet light (UV) inhibitors added to their formulations to keep the finish in the can from turning an unattractive yellow and to slow the natural aging effect of sunlight on wood.

FLOOD THE SURFACE. **The first coat will soak into the bare wood, so check the piece carefully for dry spots after it's been covered entirely. Re-coat areas that dry in the first 10 minutes or so.**

RUB OFF THE EXCESS. **Pay close attention to the inside corners and the areas around details like cock beading, where the finish can collect. It's more difficult to remove excess finish after it has hardened.**

All varnishes are naturally glossy. The softer luster of a satin or semigloss varnish results from the addition of a flattening agent, such as aluminum stearate or silica, which breaks up the reflection of light off the wood's surface. Stick with a gloss for the toughest finish, and use steel wool to get a satin finish, if that's what you're after.

Boiled Linseed or Tung Oil and Turpentine

For the oil component of my finish, I use either boiled linseed oil or tung oil (also known as China wood oil). Boiled linseed oil is made by steam-heating processed oil from raw flax and adding metallic drier compounds. The nondrying portion of the oil is removed, making what's left suitable as a finish.

Tung oil also is heat-treated, which speeds its curing time when exposed to oxygen. Tung oil is more expensive than linseed oil. However, it cures to a tougher, more water-resistant film, and it doesn't darken the wood as much. If you want maximum protection and a light color, use tung oil. Don't use raw linseed oil because it won't dry.

I thin my varnish and oil finish with turpentine. This increases surface penetration and speeds drying time. High-quality turpentine is getting harder and harder to find. It largely has been replaced by mineral spirits, which should work. I stick with turpentine because it's always worked well for me.

BRUSH ON SUBSEQUENT COATS, ONE AREA AT A TIME. Keep checking areas you've already coated to see whether they've started to become tacky. After the first coat, the finish becomes sticky quickly.

TWO RAGS ARE BETTER THAN ONE. To remove excess finish after each coat, the author uses two rags. The first one picks up the majority of the residual finish; the second ensures the wood is really dry.

Brush It On; Rub It Off

The key to a really good finish with this mixture, or any finish for that matter, is to prepare the surface well. For me, this usually means a planed or scraped surface. I find this to be faster and more enjoyable than sanding. If you do sand, start with a fairly coarse grit, and work up to at least 220 grit. But it's less important which grit you end up with than how thoroughly you work through each grit to eliminate scratches from the previous grit.

For the first coat of finish, I brush on the mixture, flooding the surface and re-coating any dry areas that appear (see the bottom left photo on p. 76). After half an hour or less, any finish still on the surface will start to feel tacky. As soon as it does, I start rubbing with clean cotton rags to absorb it (see the bottom right photo on p. 76).

This initial coat is the easiest to apply because most of it soaks right in. Nevertheless, it's important to wipe off every bit of excess so that the surface doesn't turn into a sticky mess. When the surface is thoroughly rubbed dry, I'll set it aside for at least 24 hours before re-coating. Make sure you dispose of the rags properly. Either spread them flat outside until they've dried or put them in a metal bucket with a lid. Oily rags can combust spontaneously.

Subsequent coats of finish go on in the same way, except that they tack up more quickly and require more rubbing to remove the excess. How fast these coats tack up depends on the temperature and humidity and on the type and amount of varnish in the mixture. Polyurethane varnishes cure within a few hours and can tack up very quickly; spar varnish can take twice as long.

When finishing a large piece of furniture, I work on one section at a time. I keep checking the areas I've already coated so that when the finish begins to tack up, I can start rubbing immediately (see the photo on p. 77). If I happen to get behind, brushing on a fresh coat of finish softens the tacky layer enough so that I can rub it down.

I like to use two rags, one for most of the excess finish and one for a final once-over polish (see the photo at left). Any places that aren't wiped clean will feel crusty. I don't worry about these too much because I can either rub them down with steel wool or rub especially vigorously when wiping off the next coat of finish.

How many coats to apply is a matter of choice and good judgment. Each layer adds a little more depth to the finish, some gloss, and some additional protection. For a chest of drawers, three coats is fine. For a table that's going to see hard use, I would go with a minimum of four coats—five would be better. When I'm satisfied with the finish, I wait at least 24 hours, and then I top it off with a paste wax made from beeswax, boiled linseed oil, and turpentine (see the sidebar at right).

Using the Finish to Fill the Grain

Another one of the beauties of this finish is that open-grained woods such as red oak or ash don't need to be filled before finishing. Lightly sanding the wet finish with 220-grit (or finer) sandpaper smooths the surface and creates a pore-filling slurry. I usually apply the first coat in the usual manner and sand the mixture after applying it for the second and third coats.

This method is easier than using a filler, and there are no problems with compatibility or bonding between the layers of finish. I avoid wet-or-dry, silicon-carbide sandpaper because the dark abrasive can color the pores. Instead, I use garnet or aluminum-oxide abrasives.

Rejuvenating the Finish Is Easy

If the finish needs repair or if it just starts to look tired, it's easy to fix. First clean the surface well with 0000 steel wool, turpentine and a little boiled linseed oil, and then wipe the surface until the rags come clean. A light sanding with 320-grit sandpaper will take care of any stubborn areas the steel wool can't handle. Apply a fresh coat of finish, and rub it out with clean rags. After the finish has fully cured, reapply a wax topcoat.

GARRETT HACK designs and builds furniture in Thetford Center, Vt.

Beeswax Topcoat

My favorite topcoat is made of a combination of beeswax, boiled linseed oil, and turpentine. This mixture is not as hard as a paste wax made with carnauba, but it's durable enough and it smells great.

In a double boiler on very low heat, I melt together a hunk of light-yellow beeswax (saved from comb honey I bought from a local beekeeper) and slightly less than equal amounts of oil and turpentine. I aim for a consistency similar to butter warmed to room temperature. It should be soft while maintaining its shape (see the inset photo above). If the wax mixture cools to something harder or softer than this, I add more oil or wax, whichever is appropriate, and re-warm. This recipe is very forgiving.

I apply the wax with 0000 steel wool, rubbing out the cured final coat of my oil-varnish mixture at the same time (see the top photo). If the wax is the right consistency, it smooths out easily without feeling gummy. After a few minutes of drying, I buff it with a clean rag to a satin sheen (see the photo on p. 75). To maintain the finish, just re-wax.

Wiped-On Varnish

BY THOMAS E.
WISSHACK

The use of a bristle brush for applying varnish is so commonplace that many woodworkers don't realize there is any other way. We tend to think of varnish as a traditional finish that must be applied in fairly heavy coats, usually with a brush. This is actually a myth. Some of the oldest and most beautiful finishes relied on numerous, thin coats of varnish that were rubbed onto the wood surface with a soft cloth and then polished to a delightful shine. I believe wiped-on varnish is an important addition to any wood finisher's arsenal of methods. I also think it's the most useful and versatile technique for creating a beautiful finish. The advantages of using a wiped-on finish are all related to the fact that the individual coats are extremely thin and dry quickly. Let's look at a few of these positive features.

Minimal dust contamination

Dust contamination is a major drawback for people brushing varnish; it dries so slowly foreign particles have plenty of time to land in it. But when the varnish is wiped on, the individual coats of varnish dry rapidly, so dirt doesn't have much chance to adhere. This is an enormous advantage for the wood finisher, because most of the time spent perfecting a varnish finish is a direct result of dust and foreign particles becoming embedded in it.

Minimal application marks

Though varnish can be made to flow and level nicely when brushed on, it's hard to achieve a flawless surface without some sanding. If applied properly, a wiped-on varnish virtually eliminates runs, sags, and application marks. The marks that do exist are much easier to remove because the finish layer is thin.

Less buildup

It's rarely necessary to build a thick layer of varnish. Aesthetically, a thinner application is more appealing. By wiping on the varnish, you have infinite control over the final thickness because you can apply as many or as few coats as you want.

Candidates for a Wiped-On Finish

It's difficult to build up a wiped-on varnish finish to a thickness suitable for a much-used kitchen table or bar top. I've used it on small tables, chests of drawers, frames, boxes, woodwork, and numerous other projects that don't normally receive hard use and aren't exposed to spillage or constant moisture. But I don't want to give the impression that wiped-on varnish is not durable.

I've used it, with multiple coats, on dining room tabletops where an elegant finish was required. A wiped-on finish will hold up remarkably well, provided a certain amount of common sense is used in caring for it. For example, a wiped-on finish resists mild abrasion and occasional spillage, but if you plan to place a hot dish on the surface or expect it to resist deep scratches, you'd be better off with some other type of finish.

Remember that the number of coats you wipe on has a tremendous effect on the durability of the finish. One or two coats will afford only marginally more protection than several applications of a Danish-type oil finish. Six to 10 wipe-on coats begin to approach the durability of a single thickness of varnish applied with a brush. Determine

ACHIEVE A TRADITIONAL LOOK
with multiple, thin coats and lots of
elbow grease for the final polish.

Step 1: The Sealer

THE IMPORTANT THING IS TO WORK THE SEALER–two parts thinner to one part varnish–into the wood. A natural bristle brush works well. After the surface is completely coated, wipe off all the sealer with a rag.

whether you are willing to spend the time a wiped-on varnish finish requires. The very nature of the process causes you to slow down and approach the finishing of your project with care.

Most Varnishes Can Be Wiped On

Virtually any kind of varnish can be applied with a cloth. It's simply a matter of learning a particular varnish's characteristics and developing a technique for applying it successfully.

FOR THE FINISH COATS, MAKE A FINISHER'S BALL. Make a pillow of cotton cloth filled with cheese-cloth, and hold the ball together with a rubber band. A shallow pan makes a good vessel for dipping varnish.

Polyurethane is a good example. Strikingly beautiful finishes can be created by wiping on some polyurethanes, but polyurethane is normally thicker than standard varnish, and it takes a little more practice to master. Waterborne varnish can be built up in many layers with a cloth and rubbed to a lustrous sheen, though it tends to dry very quickly when wiped on, which limits its use to relatively small projects. Certain tung oil varnishes, sold as wiping varnishes, are actually designed for cloth application and have a consistency that makes them appropriate for a good finish.

The real prerequisite for a varnish that is to be wiped on is the hardness and durability of the film it leaves on the wood's surface. Because the final layer of finish is much thinner than a brushed-on varnish finish, it only makes sense for you to work with a high-quality, brand-name product.

Certain precautions should be taken to reduce dust in your finishing area. If at all possible, do the finishing in a separate room of your shop. This is not always practical, but you can still minimize the problem by raising your work off the ground, cleaning the area and sprinkling the surrounding floor with water. Wet a 10-ft. area around your project, as well as the path you will be using to exit the shop. For small projects, you can

Step 2: The Varnish Coats

START WITH THE INTRICATE DETAILS, AND FINISH THE TOP LAST. For the detailed parts of furniture—legs, pedestals, carved pieces—it's not always possible to wipe on the varnish with the grain of the wood. Quick coverage and a gentle touch with the finisher's ball are what's important to avoid drips and runs.

COVER SURFACE QUICKLY, AND THEN GO WITH THE GRAIN. For the finish coats of wiped-on varnish, you have to work fast before the varnish dries. After you've covered the surface with varnish, land the ball at one edge, taking a light stroke with the wood grain. Lift the ball from the surface just before you get to the far edge. It takes a little practice.

build a cardboard hood over the finish area, or you can place a cardboard box over a small object while it dries. Vacuum the cardboard box, and mist the inside with water before placing it over your project.

Brush on the Sealer

The first step in a wiped-on finish is sealing the wood. The sealer coat makes the finish coats glide on more smoothly, and it results in a smoother, more professional-looking final product. Whatever varnish you plan to use will make a good sealer. Thin the varnish with two parts of high-quality mineral spirits or turpentine. Avoid thinning varnish with naphtha because the naphtha will cause the sealer to dry too quickly.

Apply the sealer with a natural bristle brush to one section of your project at a time. Use the product liberally, making sure everything is covered. Work it into the pores of the wood in all directions. Let it soak in about one minute, and then remove all superfluous varnish with cloths.

It's wise to let this sealer coat dry overnight—two days is even better—before attempting to apply subsequent coats of finish. This ensures that the surface you're working with is completely dry. A distinct advantage of the sealer coat is that it stabilizes the moisture content in the wood, allowing the subsequent coats to level and dry much more reliably.

Third Step Is Leveling

AFTER THE LAST COAT OF VARNISH AND BEFORE THE FINAL POLISHING, the author levels the surface with 600-grit paper, a foam sanding block, and a little water. It takes a light touch. The intent is to knock off dust or debris that might have dried into the varnish despite precautionary measures.

The Dance of the Finisher's Ball

The ideal applicator for wiping on varnish is a wood finisher's ball made from a soft cotton cloth filled with cheesecloth, forming a small pillow. A rubber band holds the ball together and makes a convenient handle.

Before you use the varnish, be sure to strain it through a cone-shaped painter's strainer or a piece of lint-free cheesecloth stretched across the top of an empty can. Dilute the varnish to a 50/50 mixture with the same thinner that you used for the sealer.

Then pour the mixture into a thin aluminum pan such as the type pot pies come in.

Dip your finisher's ball into the mixture, and then tap the sides of the pan lightly so that nothing is actually dripping from your cloth. I always start with the smaller, more intricately detailed parts of a piece of furniture before I finish the large planes. When I applied finish to the table shown in the photos, I started with the pedestal and legs and finished the tabletop last.

Apply the finish in a circular motion, and don't worry about neatness at first. You will need to work quickly because the thinly applied coats dry rapidly. Next use long, gliding movements, holding the wood finisher's ball in the air and landing it lightly on the wood's surface.

Work with deft strokes in the direction of the wood grain. At the far end of a flat surface, lift the ball from the surface just as you come to the edge. Repeat until you have deposited a smooth, continuous layer of varnish. Dip into the pan for fresh varnish when your cloth becomes dry or begins to drag. When you are finished with a large flat surface, such as a tabletop, dip the ball into the varnish mixture, and gently apply a coat of varnish to the top's edges.

It's a good idea to let a coat of varnish dry overnight before applying the next coat. Here's a quick test for dryness: Lightly stroke a surface with your finest paper. If the paper produces a white powder on the surface of the wood, it's dry enough and ready for the next coat.

Possible Pitfalls

Here are a few of the common problems that can occur when applying varnish with a cloth, along with appropriate solutions.

Varnish dries before a coat can be successfully applied You may need to practice on small boards before attempting a large piece of furniture. It takes a little time

Final Step Is Polishing

UNFOLD A PAD OF 0000 STEEL WOOL, AND DRY RUB ALL SURFACES TO A DULL SHEEN. Then mix mineral oil and powered rottenstone into a slurry, and rub the steel wool for several minutes more. If the slurry seems dry and too abrasive, add more oil.

WIPE WITH COTTON CLOTHS TO REMOVE OIL AND ROTTENSTONE. Continue changing soiled cloths until the cloth stays clean when you wipe the surfaces.

to learn to apply the finish quickly and evenly. It's also possible that your varnish is drying so quickly that you don't have enough time to apply a thin coat. Try thinning the varnish slightly, increasing the amount of solvent in very small increments until it seems to be easier to work with. If a particular finish continues to give you trouble, switch to another brand.

Finish appears streaky and uneven or has rough areas Roughness usually means you have overworked the varnish and portions of it have begun to dry. Don't

go back in and tamper with it. If an application is extremely rough, remove it right away with solvent rather than attempt to sand it smooth when dry.

Varnish takes several days to dry or stays gummy Chances are, the sealer coat was not given ample drying time, and trapped moisture is affecting your finish. This is common in damp weather, but it can also be caused by wood moisture. Put the object in a warm, dry place. If it does not begin to dry after 24 hours, scrub the piece with 0000 steel wool and naphtha.

A wiped-on finish will hold up remarkably well, provided a certain amount of common sense is used in caring for it.

Wipe off all bad finish, let the piece dry overnight, and reapply the sealer. Wait several days; then apply the wiped-on coats as usual.

How Many Coats?

For wiped-on finish to be at all durable, four coats should be thought of as a minimum; beyond that, it depends upon the look you are trying to achieve. I sometimes apply six to 10 individual coats to a small project, such as a box made of exotic or unusual wood. I have applied as many as 20 coats to very special projects. More coats give greater depth to the wood surface and are ideal when you want to show off a particularly handsome piece of wood. Keep in mind that with practically any varnish, regardless of whether it is marketed as semigloss or satin, the gloss will increase, and the grain will begin to fill when multiple coats are applied.

The Final Rub

Let the final coat of varnish dry about two days before attempting to do any rubbing. Less time could cause a too-soft finish to be ruined; more time could cause it to harden to the point where it's difficult to rub out. There are two very important steps to the rubbing-out process: leveling and polishing.

Even a flawlessly applied wipe-on finish will need a little sandpaper leveling to remove the tiniest specks of dust that might have accumulated in the finish when it was drying. If you attempted to rub such a finish with steel wool alone, the abrasive would ride over high spots caused by debris and create a superficially smooth, yet bumpy surface. Leveling cuts through these high spots and prepares the finish for the polishing of the surface.

I use new 600-grit wet-or-dry sandpaper, lubricated with a few drops of water. A soft rubber sanding block keeps fingers from digging in and aids in the leveling process. Keep in mind that a few strokes is often enough to do the job. Avoid too much pressure on the ends of boards. It's fairly easy to damage a thin finish, though using the 600-grit paper makes this less likely.

Polishing is the final step in producing a superior wiped-on finish. Open a pad of 0000 steel wool to maximum size, and begin rubbing dry along the wood grain in long, even strokes. Stop before you run over the edge of the surface you are rubbing to avoid going through the finish where it is vulnerable. Rub until the surface has been uniformly dulled down, using only moderate pressure. The process will take several minutes per section. Stop frequently to examine your progress using a light held obliquely to the surface.

When the surfaces have a dull sheen, lubricate the steel wool with mineral oil and rottenstone to make a slurry, and continue rubbing in the direction of the grain for two or three minutes. This evens out any streakiness that is a result of the dry rubbing. Also, it leaves the surface, when wiped down, with a very attractive semidull sheen that will not smudge or remain oily. Special rubbing lubricants for wood finishing are made, but after trying them all, including paraffin, I find mineral oil the least greasy and easiest to remove completely.

After a few minutes of rubbing, use a clean cotton cloth to remove the rottenstone and the oil, wiping with the grain and changing cloths when they get soiled. When the cloth remains clean, picking up no more oil or rottenstone, the finish is, at last, finished. Beautiful!

THOMAS E. WISSHACK makes and restores furniture in Galesburg, Ill.

A No-Brainer Varnish Technique

About a year ago, I moved my refinishing business. This time around, I was determined to install the most up-to-date spray booth right from the start. Though assured by the designer that it would be up and running within a month after moving into the new shop, inevitable delays stretched that timetable into several months. Somehow I had to keep a furniture-restoration business running that had a reputation of providing a quick turnaround on jobs.

Until the new booth was in order, spraying was out of the question, so I had to come up with a quick-dry finishing system. After some trial and error, I developed a method of wiping on a fast-dry varnish with a paper towel. The varnish provided protective qualities similar to those of a standard nitrocellulose lacquer. It was easy to apply, and it dried fast enough that all the dust kicked up by workmen wasn't a problem. I was so impressed with the results that this technique is now a staple in my teaching repertoire, and students love the results.

BY JEFF JEWITT

UNORTHODOX, BUT IT WORKS. This simple method, which uses fast-drying varnish and smooth-textured paper towels, solved the author's need to apply a quick-drying, long-lasting finish.

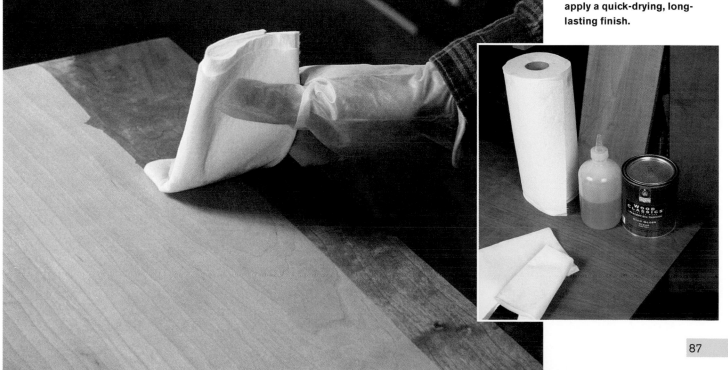

This Finish Is Easy to Apply and Dries Fast Without Dust

The Piece

SIX COATS IN TWO DAYS. After sanding this small table through 180 grit, it took less than a day to apply the first three coats of diluted, fast-dry varnish.

Step 1

FOLD IT UP AND SQUIRT. Glue bottles make great dispensers for the thinned finish. Replenish the supply of finish as necessary to keep it flowing smoothly onto the surface of the wood.

Materials

FAST-DRY VARNISHES WORK BEST. These three brands dry so fast that you can apply a second or third coat within hours of the first one.

USE A SMOOTH-TEXTURED PAPER TOWEL. The author prefers Viva brand towels. Heavily textured paper towels can leave streaks in the finish.

Step 2

LAY IT ON IN LONG STROKES WITH A LITTLE OVERLAP.
Wipe on the finish in long strokes in the direction of
the grain. Each successive stroke overlaps the previous
one by about ½ in. Work from one side of a piece to the
other, always rubbing in the same direction. Take care
to dispose of used paper towels properly.

Step 3

STRIVE FOR A LIGHT TOUCH.
Scuff-sand the dried finish
very lightly. A sufficiently
dried finish will turn to
powder; one that's too wet
will form gumballs on the
sandpaper.

Step 4

REDUCE THE SHEEN WITH STEEL WOOL. Using very fine
(0000) steel wool, you can turn a gloss finish into a satin
sheen by rubbing the final coat of varnish with the direction
of the grain.

After a week's drying time you can rub out the finish if that's the look you want.

What to Use

Fast-dry varnishes are similar to typical alkyd varnishes, but the drying time is sped up by adding vinyl toluene to the alkyd resin. These varnishes dry tack-free in as little as 15 minutes. This means that the conventional problem associated with varnish—dust drying in the finish—is eliminated. The three brands I've used—Zinsser's Quick-15, Sherwin Williams' Wood Classics Fast-Dry Oil Varnish and Benjamin Moore's One Hour Clear Finish—are available in gloss and satin versions. I use gloss for this technique because satin versions tend to dry a bit streaky when applied in thin coats. Gloss can also be rubbed down to satin, as I'll explain later.

When brushing on varnish, bubbles sometimes form in the finish. But by thinning the varnish and wiping it on with a paper towel, bubbles are eliminated. Any nontextured paper towel will work, but my favorite brand is Viva. Avoid textured paper towels.

I use naphtha to thin varnish because it dries the fastest; I can easily apply three coats in a day. Mineral spirits will extend the drying time, so you'll probably be able to apply only two coats a day.

How to Do It

Sand the wood through 180 grit. I use a random-orbit sander and then hand-sand with the grain, using the same grit. Remove all sawdust and other debris, and then apply any stain you want. Allow the stain to dry. Dismantle the project as much as you can so that you have flat surfaces to finish. Thin the varnish with equal parts naphtha or mineral spirits and put the thinned solution into a plastic squeeze bottle with a dispensing nozzle—the type you find on a glue bottle.

Fold a single piece of paper towel once perpendicular to the perforated seam. Fold it again perpendicular to the previous fold, then fold it again. You should end up with a rectangular piece of folded towel approximately 2¾ in. by 5 in.

Hold the paper towel so that the tip extends just beyond your fingers and apply a squirt of varnish (about ¼ oz.) to the tip of the towel. Bring the towel down onto the surface of the workpiece and wipe a thin, even coat from one edge to the other. Don't bear down too hard at the beginning or you'll get a pool of finish. Replenish the towel again and make another swipe, overlapping the first one by about ½ in. or so. Repeat this process until you've covered the whole surface. Do the edges last. The thin varnish sets up quickly, allowing you to fix a drip immediately. But your goal should be to get the varnish on as evenly and as quickly as you can and then leave it alone.

The first coat should be dry enough to sand in about an hour. Use 400-grit silicon-carbide sandpaper and scuff the surface just enough to remove any nibs. If the varnish film turns to powder easily when you sand it, then it is dry enough to re-coat. Remove the dust with a tack rag and apply the second coat just like the first. After a few hours, scuff-sand and apply a third coat.

After overnight drying, sand the finish again with 400-grit paper. Wipe all of the residue with a tack rag and build at least two more coats, and as many more as you like. When the finish depth is to your liking, stop. I typically apply six coats to maximize durability.

After a week's drying time you can rub out the finish if that's the look you want. Wet-sand the finish lightly with 600-grit wet-or-dry paper, by hand. Then, using 0000 steel wool and wax thinned with mineral spirits, rub the finish with the grain in long strokes. This results in a very pleasant satin sheen.

JEFF JEWITT is a contributor to *Fine Woodworking* magazine and the author of *Taunton's Complete Illustrated Guide to Finishing*.

Padding Lacquer

BY MARIO RODRIGUEZ

For me, French polishing is the finish of choice for the very finest furniture. When done well, a French polish has a soft but brilliant glow that brings out all the depth and color of the wood without the heavy buildup generally associated with a high-gloss finish. No other finish even comes close.

I've taught French polishing for years, and for beginners, it can be a nerve-racking juggling act. The ingredients of a French polish—shellac, oil, and pumice—must be applied at the right time and in the proper amounts. The addition of each can improve the finish dramatically—or destroy it. Padding lacquer is an amazing one-step mixture of dissolved shellac, lubricants and nitrocellulose resins. It produces a surface virtually identical to that of a traditional French polish, without the risks. It still

Surface Preparation

1 SCRAPE THE SURFACE until it's flat and even in appearance.

2 SAND WITH THE GRAIN using 220- and then 320-grit sandpaper.

requires a lot of elbow grease, but because it's a premixed formula, you can concentrate on applying it and not worry about maintaining a delicate balance of ingredients. There are several brands of padding lacquers from which to choose (see Sources on p. 95). I haven't found significant differences among them.

In addition to being convenient and easy to apply, padding lacquer dries quickly, so you don't need a special finishing room. It can even be applied on-site, eliminating the need to bring a piece of furniture back to the shop for finish repairs. And because shellac is the primary ingredient in a padding lacquer, it can be applied over other finishes. Finally, padding lacquer has a variable sheen. The more or less sanding you do will increase or decrease its gloss.

Surface Preparation

For more formal furniture pieces, which generally look best with a high-gloss finish like a French polish, I scrape the wood until I have a fairly flat, uniform surface (see the top photo at left). Then I sand with 220-grit and 320-grit sandpaper (see the bottom photo at left).

After wiping the surface with a dry rag, I wash it down with denatured alcohol. This raises the grain slightly and allows me to see sanding scratches and any other flaws (see the first photo on the facing page). If I want to fill the pores slightly for a smoother finish, I wet-sand with worn 320-grit wet-or-dry sandpaper and denatured alcohol. If I want a glass-smooth, nonporous finish, I use a filler (see the sidebar on p. 94). For a moderately porous, more natural-looking finish, just dry-sand with 320- and 400-grit sandpapers once the denatured alcohol has dried.

Applying Padding Lacquer

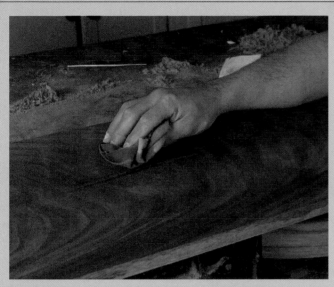

1 CHECK FOR SANDING SCRATCHES AND OTHER FLAWS by flooding the surface with denatured alcohol. This also raises the grain slightly, so follow up by sanding with 320- and then 400-grit sandpaper.

2 QUICK, CIRCULAR MOTIONS BRING UP A SHINE. Move the pad in tight circles in a small area, applying a good deal of pressure. The surface will be hazy at first, but after just a minute or so, a shine will start to come up. Apply less pressure as the shine increases.

3 WORK JUST A FEW SQUARE INCHES AT A TIME, blending adjacent areas. Apply more pressure on unfinished areas.

4 POLISH THE WHOLE SURFACE LIGHTLY. Take a clean rag, apply just a little padding lacquer, and rub very lightly. The rag should just skate across the surface. Do this until the whole surface has a uniform sheen.

Pore Filler
Gives a Glass-Smooth Surface

In traditional French polishing, pumice helps fill the pores in the surface. Padding lacquer has no pumice, so the pores don't get filled appreciably, except by the padding lacquer itself. The result, depending on how much sanding you've done, is a relatively open-pored surface. To get a glassy-looking, nonporous surface with padding lacquer, I use Behlen's pore-filling compound called Pore-O-Pac paste wood filler (see Sources on the facing page). Pore-O-Pac is available in six shades.

Applying the filler couldn't be easier. I pour some on the surface I'm going to polish and wipe it all around with a rag (see the top left photo below). Then I use a scraper like a squeegee, moving the filler across the wood in all directions. This works the filler into the pores.

I let the filler remain on the surface between 30 minutes and one hour before wiping it off. This filler dries rock-hard, so it's important to clean the scraper and the surface you're filling. Otherwise, it will take a belt sander to remove it. I use a clean rag and keep wiping until the rag comes off the surface without any residue.

I wait 24 hours for the surface to dry, and then I fine-sand with 320- and 400-grit sandpaper. After sanding, I wipe down the surface with a rag soaked in denatured alcohol.

I let the surface dry and start applying the padding lacquer. A brilliant gloss will start to come up almost immediately.

POUR IT ON, SMEAR IT AROUND. You don't have to be fussy when applying wood filler–just fill all the pores. Move the rag around; then use a scraper.

LIKE A MIRROR. With its pores filled, this crotch mahogany panel takes on a finish that's a dead-ringer for French polish–a warm but brilliant sheen.

FILLED PORES, SATIN SHEEN. Paste wood filler dries to a satin sheen even before padding lacquer is applied. The filler dries rock-hard, so wipe the surface clean.

Applying Padding Lacquer

When using padding lacquer, all you need is a 6-in. square of lint-free cotton. Old T-shirt scraps work great. Just make sure that there aren't any creases or seams in the center of the pad because they can mar your finish.

I pour a small amount of padding lacquer into the center of my cloth and let it soak in a few seconds. Then with a small, circular motion, I begin to rub the polish vigorously into the surface (see the second photo on p. 93). Initially, the surface will haze and the cloth will drag a little, but with firm, steady pressure, an attractive shine will quickly start to appear. As I move from one small area to another, I carefully overlap my applications for uniform coverage (see the third photo on p. 93).

A second coat can be applied almost immediately. As you build up the polish, though, you should extend the time between coats for the best results. When I get to my fourth and fifth coats, I usually wait between 12 and 24 hours.

Feathering Out the Finish

Even with very careful application, some areas will have more of a sheen than others, and the overall surface may look splotchy. You'll want to go over duller areas and make the surface as uniform as possible.

Then put a small amount of padding lacquer on a clean rag, and apply it over the entire surface, using a broad, circular motion. Bring the cloth just barely into contact with the work surface—almost glancing over it. This will eliminate any small streaks or blotches and leave a consistently brilliant, thin film (see the fourth photo on p. 93).

Repairing Mistakes

As easy as padding lacquer is to use, I do run into small problems from time to time. These problems usually appear as rough crater-like patches. If they're not too severe, I simply pad over them. The application of new material usually will soften the area and vigorous rubbing will level it out. If this doesn't do the trick, I'll let the panel dry overnight, scrape or sand the damaged area flush the next day, and then repolish. After a coat or two, blemishes will disappear completely.

Finishing on the Lathe

I often use padding lacquer on lathe-turned objects, including table pedestals, spindles, cabinet knobs, and tool handles. Here the application is even easier. Sand to 320 grit with the object spinning on the lathe. Then raise the grain with alcohol, and sand again with 320- and then 400-grit paper. You can apply the padding lacquer a little more heavily on the lathe, but don't use so much that it's spraying off the workpiece. Use gentle pressure on the rotating workpiece, and watch an incredible gloss develop.

MARIO RODRIGUEZ teaches woodworking at the Fashion Institute of Technology in New York City. He is a contributing editor to *Fine Woodworking* magazine.

Sources

Garrett Wade
161 Avenue of the Americas
New York, NY 10013
800-221-2942

Woodworker's Supply, Inc.
1108 N. Glenn Road
Casper, WY 82601
800-645-9292

Industrial Finishing Products
465 Logan St.
Brooklyn, NY 11208
718-277-3333

Padding On Shellac

BY JEFF JEWITT

Padding shellac is a low-tech process that is perfectly suited to the professional and amateur finisher. The advantages of shellac are numerous. It is a nontoxic, Food and Drug Administration-approved natural resin. The carrier for shellac, ethanol, is relatively nontoxic (ethanol is the same kind of alcohol that's found in liquor), and the fumes are not unpleasant. Shellac dries quickly, so dust does not pose a great problem, and finishes can be done in two to three days.

Applying shellac by padding it on is an easy technique to master. I rub on a freshly dissolved shellac solution over a sealer coat of oil, which increases the finish depth. I let each coat dry overnight and continue rubbing on shellac until I've achieved the

desired depth and gloss I'm after. Shellac is a good-looking, durable finish that can easily be repaired if damaged. But because shellac can be dissolved by alcohol, this finish is not a good choice for a bar top.

The materials for padding shellac are inexpensive and easy to obtain through most finishing companies (see Sources on p. 100). They consist of shellac, denatured alcohol, padding cloth, a drying oil such as boiled linseed oil or tung oil, sandpaper, and synthetic steel wool.

The Materials

I prefer to make my own shellac solution of 2 lb. of dry shellac flakes dissolved in a gallon of alcohol (a 2-lb. cut; see the sidebar on p. 98). Using fresh shellac will help you

SHELLAC IN DRY FORM IS AVAILABLE IN A VARIETY OF GRADES. Seedlac (1) and buttonlac (2) are among the least refined forms of shellac. The most common shellac is #1 orange (3). The next two are more highly refined dewaxed shellacs, available in dark-golden brown (4) and pale amber (5). Bleached white shellac (6) yields a colorless solution.

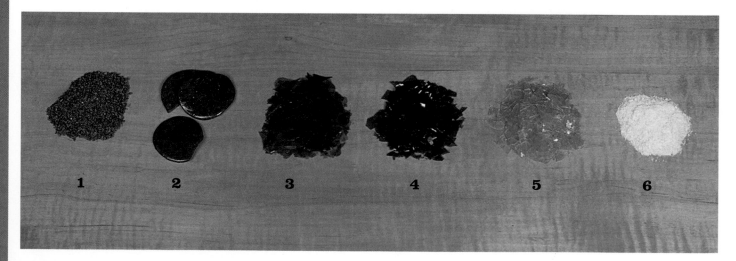

1   2   3   4   5   6

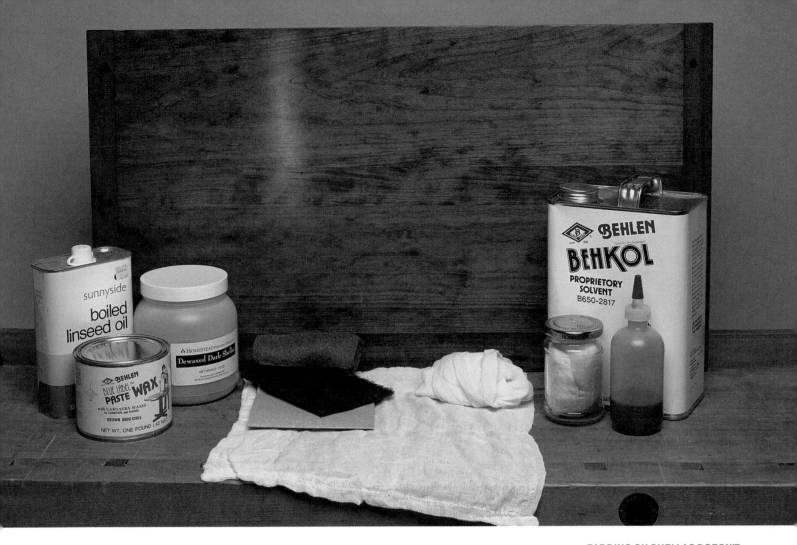

avoid one of the classic complaints against shellac as a finish—it won't dry. Shellac is made up of organic acids that react with alcohol in a process called esterification. This gradual reaction produces esters, gummy substances that inhibit drying in old shellac.

Although it's possible to use premixed shellac, any liquid shellac older than six months should be tested for drying problems. (Wm. Zinsser Co. makes shellac with a longer shelf life.) To test shellac, place a drop or two on a piece of glass. If it's not dry to the touch in five minutes, don't use it. Premixed shellac is available only in orange or white (chemically bleached) varieties; there are more choices if you buy it in dry form (see the photo on the facing page). And if you mix your own shellac, you are guaranteed a fresh solution.

There are four alcohol solvents for shellac—methanol, ethanol, butanol and propanol. Methanol is an excellent solvent,

but it's extremely poisonous. The fumes will pass through organic vapor respirators, so I avoid using methanol in my shop. Ethanol is far better because of its low toxicity. Butanol has an odor I find disagreeable, so I don't use it as the main solvent. I do add it occasionally to ethanol-reduced shellac as a retarder because butanol's higher molecular weight makes it evaporate slightly more slowly than ethanol. Propanol, the alcohol in rubbing alcohol, can be hard to get in chemically pure form. Don't use rubbing alcohol to dissolve shellac; it is 30% water and will cause problems in the shellac film.

An excellent product made specifically for reducing shellac is a Behlen product called Behkol (see Sources on p. 100), which is 95% anhydrous ethanol and 5% isobutanol. The isobutanol slows down the drying time slightly.

The best cloth for applying shellac is manufactured from bleached, 100% cotton and is sold as padding, trace, or French

PADDING ON SHELLAC DOESN'T REQUIRE LOTS OF FANCY EQUIPMENT. You can get a beautiful finish with a minimum of materials: shellac flakes, solvent, boiled linseed oil, and wax. The author finished the tabletop in the background by padding on shellac.

What's Shellac, and How Is It Used?

Shellac is derived from a natural resin secreted by a tiny insect called Laccifer lacca. This insect alights on certain trees indigenous to India and Thailand and feeds off sap in the twigs. The insects secrete a cocoon-type shell, which is harvested by workers shaking the tree branches. In this form, the resin is called sticklac and contains bits of twig, insect, and other contaminants. The sticklac is then washed to remove impurities. At this point, it may be refined either by hand or machine. The next step up is buttonlac, which is processed in India. It is reddish-brown and is sold in 1-in.- to 2-in.-wide buttons.

Seedlac is another impure form of shellac and is processed further in India for better-quality lacs or exported to other countries for further refining. White shellac is made in the United States by Wm. Zinsser Co. from imported seedlac that's dewaxed and bleached by bubbling chlorine gas through it.

Shellac grading is complex because it is a product with wide commercial applications. But the most important characteristics for woodworkers are those based on color and wax content. The best grades of shellac for finishing have less than 1% wax and are light-amber in color. Wax in shellac decreases its moisture resistance and makes it less transparent.

The most common shellac is industry-graded as #1 orange, which usually is 4% wax and is a brownish-orange color. Dewaxed shellacs can range in color from a dark-golden brown to a pale amber, as shown in the photo on p. 96. Fresh shellac is always better, so I mix my own, making just enough for the job at hand. For padding, I prefer a 2-lb. cut, which means 2 lb. of shellac flakes dissolved in a gallon of alcohol. For most projects, a pint (¼ lb. of flakes in 1 pint of alcohol) is sufficient. I mix shellac in a clean glass jar. Avoid metal cans because they will discolor the solution. Periodically shaking the jar prevents a jelly-like mass from forming at the bottom. Most shellacs take about a day to dissolve, so plan ahead. If it takes longer, the shellac may be bad. After dissolving in alcohol, lower-grade shellacs like buttonlac and seedlac always should be strained through a medium-mesh or fine-mesh filter to remove impurities.

polishing cloth. Whatever cloth you use, it should be clean, not dyed, lint-free and absorbent. Avoid old T-shirts or cheesecloth because of the lint. My favorite cloth comes in 12-in. squares and has a rumpled texture similar to surgical gauze, as shown in the photo on p. 97.

Use either boiled linseed oil or tung oil to seal the wood and to give greater depth to the finish (only a small amount is needed). I have not been able to discern a difference between the two under the shellac finish. Make sure the linseed oil is boiled, though, because raw linseed oil contains no driers and never really hardens.

Preparation

No finish can hide sloppy surface preparation. On new wood, I plane, scrape, and sand to 220 grit on highly visible surfaces. I also do as much surface preparation as I can on the project before it's glued up. For new work, I'll even apply the oil and the first coat of shellac before assembling a project. Applying at least the first coat of shellac before the piece has been glued up makes it much easier to get an even finish, even in hard to reach places.

I generally tape off tenons and other joints so that oiling doesn't contaminate the wood. If the wood is to be colored, I use water-soluble dyes before the oil sealer coat. These dyes raise the grain, so I knock down the raised fibers with maroon synthetic steel wool (equivalent to 00 steel wool or 320-grit sandpaper) after the dye dries. I prefer synthetic steel wool because it's not as likely to cut through the dye on the edges. After the wood is smoothed down, you're ready for the first finishing step.

Oiling

Oil seals the wood and gives it greater depth. On refinished pieces, you can omit this step. Oils will accentuate the figure and deepen the color of wood, particularly curly maple and cherry. I have used a variety of oils, but I like linseed and tung oil the best. Apply just enough oil to make the surface of the wood look wet (about a thimbleful per square foot), as shown in the left photo on the facing page. Do not flood the surface with oil. Apply the oil with a clean, soft cloth, and rub the surface briskly. It will penetrate quickly. After several minutes, begin applying the shellac.

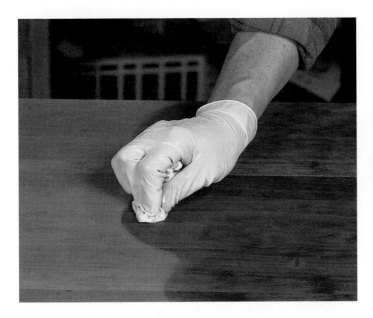

AFTER THE OIL DRIES FOR A FEW MINUTES, charge the pad with a squeeze bottle to get just the right amount of shellac. The pad should be a lint-free cloth folded so that there are no wrinkles or seams on the bottom of the pad.

FIRST APPLY A PRIMER COAT OF OIL FOR A DEEP FINISH. The author rubs in a light coat of oil, either boiled linseed or tung oil, to seal the wood. Shellac can be padded on after the oil has dried for several minutes.

Padding Shellac

Fold the padding cloth into a rolled ball, as shown in the photo on p. 97. There should be no creases or seams on the pad bottom. Pour about 1 oz. of alcohol into the pad and work it in. Then pour about ¼ oz. to ½ oz. of a 2-lb. cut shellac into the bottom of the pad. I keep my shellac in round squeeze bottles to simplify dispensing into the pad. Use just a little; you shouldn't be able to squeeze shellac from the pad.

To apply the shellac, start at the top, right-hand edge of the board, and work across the board with the grain. Bring the pad down lightly, drag it across the board and right off the opposite edge, as shown in the drawing on p. 100. Reverse directions, working back from left to right. Continue down the board, applying the shellac in alternating stripes. When you've reached the bottom, start again at the top; the board will be dry enough to repeat the process.

When the pad dries out, recharge it with more shellac. The amount of shellac you'll use depends on the size of the piece. A 24-sq.-in. piece should take about 10 or 15 minutes and will use three or four charges of shellac. On tops, do the edges first, and then continue the same sequence as above. If there is a complex molded edge, make the pad conform to the shape of the molding. The other parts of the piece (aprons, legs, and sides) get the same padding coat of shellac. When the board is tacky and the pad starts to stick, stop. Store the pad in a jar with a screw-type lid.

The first application of shellac should be dry enough to scuff-sand in approximately one hour. Using 320-grit, stearated sandpaper (aluminum oxide mixed with zinc stearate as a lubricant), lightly scuff-sand the surface. Scuff-sanding is applying just enough pressure to barely scratch the surface. After this, smooth out the surface with maroon synthetic steel wool. Then apply shellac to the other sides of all surfaces, such as the undersides of tops and the insides of carcases in the same way you did on the top.

When this coat of shellac is dry, after about an hour, scuff-sand and rub these surfaces with synthetic steel wool. After the first coat of finish has been applied, it's time to glue the project together. Be careful to avoid excess glue, and make sure that clamps are properly padded. If any glue squeezes out, you can pull it off like scotch

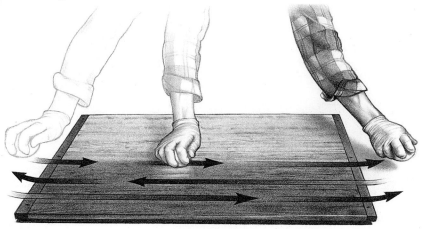

Shellac is padded on with the grain from edge to edge in an alternating pattern until the piece has been covered. The stroke should start off the edge of the board, continue across the board and off the opposite side. Stop when the finish becomes tacky, and the pad begins to stick.

Sources

The following companies manufacture or supply dry shellac flakes in various grades, padding cloth, alcohol solvents, oil, and other finishing products.

Mohawk Finishing Products, Inc.
H. Behlen & Bros.
Route 30 N.
Amsterdam, NY 12010
518-843-1380

Garrett Wade Co., Inc.
161 Avenue of the Americas
New York, NY 10013
800-221-2942

Homestead Finishing Products
P. O. Box 370275
Cleveland, OH 44136

tape after 30 minutes to an hour. Don't let the glue dry completely, it may pull off the finish when you try to remove it.

The next day, once the piece is glued up, the finishing sequence is repeated. The pad should glide easily over the surface, and you should have an even coat of shellac on the surface. As the pad starts to dry out, you can switch from polishing in a stripe pattern to a circular pattern or a series of figure-eights to get even coverage on the board. Stop when the finish is tacky and the pad sticks. At this point, the surface should have an even shine, indicating a surface build of shellac. Put the pad back in the jar, and let the finish dry overnight.

The next day, examine the finish. You should have an even coating of finish on the surface. If you are working with open-pored woods like walnut or mahogany, you'll see crisp outlines to the open pores. This level of finish is appealing to some. If so, you can stop applying shellac; simply go on to the rubbing-out stage, which I'll explain in a minute, and you're done.

For surfaces that will receive a lot of wear and tear, you may want to apply several more coats for maximum protection. If so, repeat the procedure until you've built up

the finish to the film thickness that you want, allowing each coat to dry overnight. You don't gain any added protection after four or five applications, but there is an aesthetic difference. After the final padding application, let the project dry for several days before rubbing it out.

Rubbing Out

Rubbing out the shellac finish results in a smoother, better-looking surface. The beauty of the padding application is that there are no brush marks or other surface irregularities to level, so this step usually goes quickly. The first step is to level the surface of the finish with 400-grit, wet-or-dry silicon carbide finishing paper. Then switch to 0000 steel wool, squirting mineral spirits onto the pad and dipping it into a can of paste wax.

I prefer steel wool for rubbing out because it has a better bite and leaves a better-looking finish. My favorite wax is Behlen's Blue Label paste wax, available in brown for darker finishes and natural for lighter finishes. Working with the grain, I bear down fairly hard with the steel wool and rub the wax on the surface. I wait until it begins to haze, wipe off the excess and buff to a satiny sheen. If a higher gloss is desired, rub the surface with rottenstone mixed with mineral spirits before waxing.

Maintenance

If the piece is not subjected to a lot of wear and tear, a yearly re-waxing keeps it looking great. For tables, chairs, and other high-wear items, you can rejuvenate the finish by removing the wax with mineral spirits and rubbing with maroon synthetic steel wool. Then apply a light coat of shellac, let dry, and re-wax.

JEFF JEWITT is a contributor to *Fine Woodworking* magazine and the author of *Taunton's Complete Illustrated Guide to Finishing.*

A Traditional French Polish

BY SEAN CLARKE

I became hooked on French polishing at age 15, when I apprenticed with a large firm of period furniture makers in London. I instantly wanted to pursue this incredible art form, and for the following three years I learned all aspects of the craft by studying under master French polishers.

The aim of this technique, developed in France around 1820, is to use as little material as possible to gain the most effect. It's a traditional hand finish that involves working several coats of shellac deep into the wood fibers, and the effect is one of exceptional depth and clarity. Because it is of moderate durability, a French-polished surface is best suited for display rather than hard use. But in my mind, no other finish can compare when it comes to illuminating the natural beauty inherent in wood.

As you would expect with a finish technique that is nearly 200 years old, there are many variations in the recipe, with each claiming to be the true French polish. This version has served me well for the past 18 years.

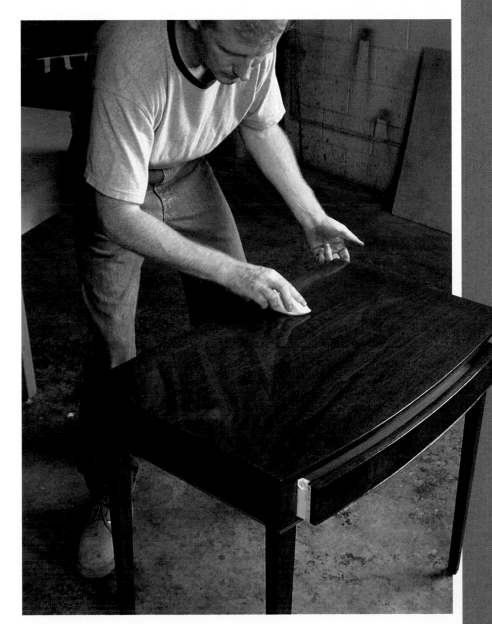

Before You Polish, Prepare the Surface

Because French polishing magnifies imperfections, good surface preparation is imperative. Begin by sanding all surfaces up to 320-grit paper. Clean off the dust, then evaluate what the finished color of the piece will be by wiping the surfaces with a cloth soaked in denatured alcohol. The Georgian-style side table shown on p. 101 was built using Honduras mahogany for the legs and frame, but the drawer, with its highly figured Cuban mahogany veneer, and the single-piece mahogany top were both salvaged from antiques beyond repair. The alcohol revealed that the legs had a pinkish hue, but the top was more orange, and the drawer front was a dark brown.

To pull the colors together, I used a mixture of water-based powdered aniline dyes: red mahogany and golden-amber maple. I applied the dye full strength to all parts of the piece except for the drawer front, where I diluted the stain. Finally, I wiped on a coat of English brown oak stain over the piece to kill the orange hue. Before you apply a stain to a piece with an inlay, apply a 2-lb. cut of super-blond shellac to the inlay using a small artist's brush to seal it, ensuring that it retains its contrast with the rest of the piece. Let everything dry.

Whether or not you stain the piece, next brush a coat of boiled linseed oil on the whole piece, then let it sit for an hour before wiping it down with a clean cloth. The oil penetrates the wood and gives maximum illumination to the fibers. Then let the piece cure for five to seven days.

Apply the First Coat of Shellac

Lightly scuff-sand all surfaces with 320-grit self-lubricating paper to knock down any raised grain and dust nibs. Next, apply a coat of super-blond shellac (2-lb. cut) to seal the dyed and oiled surface and to provide a base on which to build the finish. Be sure to use the paler super-blond shellac at this stage; a deeper-colored shellac can cause color lines and a streaky effect. I use a large-capacity badger-hair mop brush to apply the shellac to every part but the top, where I use a piece of folded cheesecloth. Apply two or three coats in the direction of the grain, then leave the workpiece to dry for a couple of hours. (I work in southern California; if you live in a more humid region, extend the drying times, as needed.)

Brush on a Pore-Filler/Glaze Mixture

Because a French-polished finish requires a uniformly smooth surface, the pores of open-grained woods, such as mahogany, need to be filled. I combine this step with a colored glaze that both harmonizes and ages the appearance. I mix my own glaze so that I can control both the color and the consistency. For this table I used the following recipe: three heaped teaspoons of burnt-umber dry pigment; one heaped teaspoon of vegetable black dry pigment; four heaped teaspoons of fine-grade pumice; 1 oz. of gold size; and 4 oz. of turpentine. Turpentine extends the shelf life of the mixture, whereas mineral spirits tends to form a gel. You can adjust the pigment colors, but do not add more pumice than pigment, which can lead to specks of gray pumice showing up in the grain.

Brush the filler/glaze mixture onto a small section at a time, then wipe it off with a clean cloth. Use a circular or figure-eight motion to remove the bulk of the liquid, then wipe across the grain to deposit more into the pores. If an area dries and becomes difficult to remove, dampen the clean cloth with turpentine. As the photo of the filled top shows (see the fourth photo

The Language of French Polishing

It is perhaps appropriate that many of the English terms for the different stages of French polishing are double entendres, a legacy perhaps of generations of master polishers embellishing the process with a mystique it doesn't deserve.

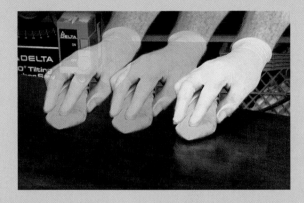

Rubber

THE TERM HAS NOTHING TO DO WITH LATEX but is derived from the method of using this tool to rub on thin layers of shellac. The exterior, known as the linen, can either be made from this fabric or more commonly from a 100% cotton sheet. The interior can be any kind of absorbent material, which also gives this tool its other name of tampon.

Floating

FLOATING IS THE PROCESS OF APPLYING SHELLAC with the rubber in straight strokes with the grain. The purpose is to achieve a firm base on which to build the body of the finish.

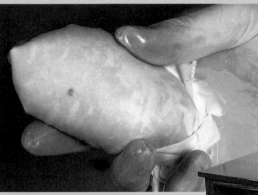

Bodying Up

THE STAGE WHERE THE BULK OF THE SHELLAC IS APPLIED to the piece is called bodying up. The rubber can either be used in a padding motion to avoid pulling away a previous layer of stain or in a swirling or figure-eight pattern. Raw linseed oil is used to lubricate the rubber and prevent it from sticking to the shellac.

Spiriting Off

THE ACTUAL POLISHING STAGE of French polishing is called spiriting off. The oil used to body up is removed by rinsing the linen of the rubber in alcohol and then lightly floating the rubber across the surface. The alcohol not only removes the oil, but it also melts the top layer of shellac, creating a smooth, high-gloss surface.

Surface Preparation Is Crucial

1 Brush on a coat of boiled linseed oil, let it soak in for an hour, and then wipe off any surplus. The oil takes at least five days to dry.

2 Using a large-capacity badger-hair mop, apply super-blond shellac in the direction of the grain.

3 Use an old brush to apply a pore-filler/glaze mixture. Because the mixture sets up fast, work on small sections at a time.

4 Work quickly before the filler dries to produce a smooth surface.

on the facing page), the glazed area is smoother and has the dark appearance of a mahogany antique.

Rub all surfaces with 0000 steel wool to remove any excess filler. In addition, wrap a turpentine-dampened cloth around a block and rub the surface to further remove any filler from the tabletop and deposit it in the pores.

There is one final step before the actual polishing can begin. After forming a rubber (see the sidebar at right), use it to float a coat of buttonlac (2-lb. cut) across the entire workpiece. Floating refers to the process of applying shellac in straight strokes with the grain. This seals in the pore filler, while the darker buttonlac deepens and enriches the color.

Polishing Starts by Bodying Up the Finish

Let the piece dry overnight, then start building up the successive shellac coats, a process called bodying up. Still using the 2-lb. cut of buttonlac, brush a couple of coats onto every part of the table but the top. Charge the rubber with shellac, then flick a few drops of raw linseed oil onto the tabletop. The oil serves as a lubricant, allowing the rubber to float smoothly across the surface, laying down coats of shellac without abrading the previous coats. I use raw linseed oil because it has a longer cure time. If the finishing needs to stretch into several days, the oil remains workable.

Apply the shellac by moving the rubber in circles and figure-eight patterns using light to moderate pressure. Recharge the rubber, as necessary, until the finish begins to build. Brush another coat onto the rest of the table, then let the piece rest for an hour.

The last thing to do is sand the piece to remove any remaining imperfections. Flick a few drops of raw linseed oil onto some 320-grit sandpaper. The oil serves as a lubricant. Use a light touch, and avoid breaking through the finish at the edges.

The Right Rubber for the Job

Every French polisher has a favorite design of rubber. If you have a preference, stick with it. For a table this size, I cut a cotton bed sheet roughly 8 in. square, removing any hems. I then cut a piece of cotton cloth approximately 6 in. square and folded it into a wad roughly 2 in. wide and 3 in. long, with a blunt point at one end.

Charge the wadding with denatured alcohol to increase its absorbency, then squirt shellac onto one surface of the wadding. Place this surface down into the center of the cloth, bring each corner of the cloth to the center, maintaining the point on one end, and twist the ends of the fabric together. Use this twist of fabric as a grip for the rubber. It is critical that the fabric be very smooth against the wadding, because this is the surface that does the polishing. Smack the rubber against the palm of your hand so that the shellac penetrates the cloth. Then you are ready to begin French polishing.

START WITH A CLEAN SHEET. Use a white 100% cotton bed sheet as the exterior, or linen, of the polishing rubber. Cut off any hemmed edges of the sheet. The cloth encloses a wadded piece of cotton.

CHARGE THE RUBBER. The shellac should be applied directly to the wadding before the rubber is used and each time it needs recharging. When not in use, store the rubber in an airtight container to prevent it from drying out.

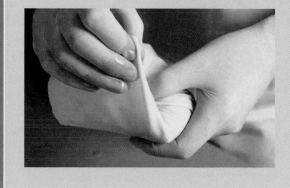

WRAP THE RUBBER CAREFULLY. The cloth should be wrapped tightly around the wadding to form a smooth surface on the bottom that will do the polishing.

Build the Finish in Layers

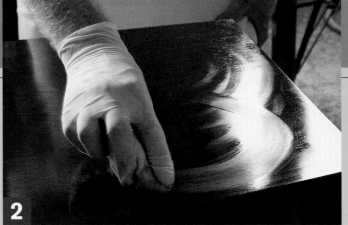

1 To apply the shellac, use a brush on all areas but the tabletop.

2 Polish the top with the rubber, using light to moderate pressure, and keep the rubber moving in circles and figure-eights.

3 Add a few drops of raw linseed oil to 320-grit paper to prevent it from biting into the finish.

4 The sandpaper is rubbed across the tabletop using the heel of the hand rather than wrapped around a block to lessen the chance of cutting through the finish on a high spot.

5 After sanding the piece, resume building the shellac finish. This time use the rubber on the whole table, not just on the top, to create a smoother surface.

6 For rubbing out the finish, unroll the steel wool so that you don't cut through the finish.

Now resume bodying up the tabletop, this time using the rubber on the legs and drawer front as well as on the tabletop. Flick the linseed oil directly onto the rubber when working on smaller areas, such as legs.

Remove the Oil by Spiriting Off

The polishing part of a French polish is variously called spiriting off or stiffing off. This step removes the previously applied oil, which if left on would leave white traces in the cured finish. The aim is to remove the oil without displacing the coats of shellac.

First wash out the cloth of the rubber in denatured alcohol, then wring it so that it is not dripping wet. Charge the wadding with a 1-lb. cut of buttonlac and rewrap the rubber. It is fine to go straight from bodying up to spiriting off without letting the finish rest.

Float the rubber across the surface of the table in straight strokes with slightly less pressure than when bodying up. The cloth of the rubber will start to pick up the oil in the finish. After going over the whole piece, rinse out the cloth in alcohol, but do not add shellac to the wadding. Float the rubber across the surface again and again, regularly rinsing out the cloth, which will become progressively drier. When you don't see any more oil being collected and the sheen has become an even gloss, stop and allow the piece to dry overnight.

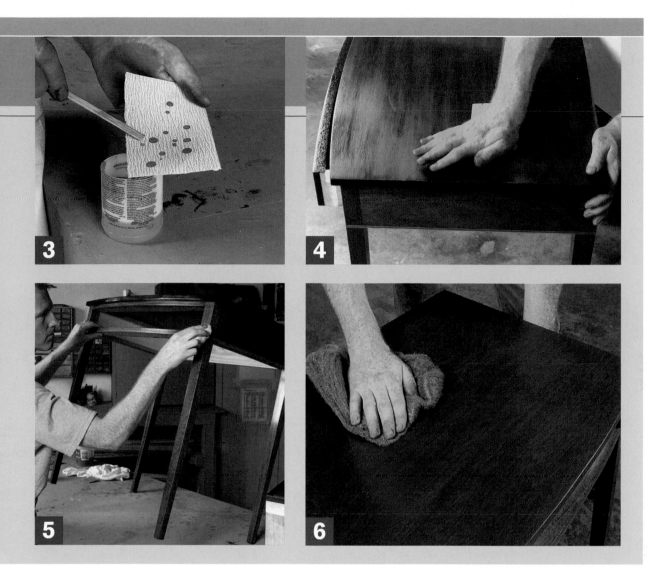

Rub Out and Compound the Finish

Your personal preference for final appearance decides the next step. For a high-gloss look, the finish must be rubbed out using 2,000-grit wet-or-dry sandpaper. I used the paper dry on the legs, the frame, and the drawer front of the table shown here, but on the top I used water as a lubricant. With a very light touch, sand in the direction of the grain and concentrate on not burning through the finish at the edges. Then apply a polishing compound in a circular motion using a clean cloth.

If you prefer a more satin level of gloss, rub the surface with 0000 steel wool. For the small areas of the table, I tore a strip of

wool down the middle and folded it into a small pad that fit my hand. For the tabletop I used a larger wad to distribute the pressure more evenly and to prevent the steel wool from becoming clogged. With this method, always rub the steel wool in the direction of the grain.

Last, Add a Coat of Wax

Because I have always had a preference for an aged appearance to reproduction furniture, I like to add the step of "blacking in" to the wax polishing. I make my own blend of polish using the following recipe: one teaspoon of vegetable black pigment; 1 oz. of slow-set gold size; 4 oz. of Kiwi Bois paste wax; and enough turpentine to

Sources

Easy Leaf Products
(slow and fast gold size)
800-569-5323
www.easyleaf.com

Homestead Finishing
(black pigment)
216-631-5309
www.homesteadfinish-ing.com

Hummer Capital Inc.
(Kiwi Bois wax)
800-552-0052
www.hummercap.com

A Homemade Aging Process

A BLACK-WAX RECIPE. The author makes his own wax polish and combines it with gold size and black pigment to give the table an aged luster.

BRUSH ON THE BLACK WAX. Using a cheap brush, apply the wax in corners and crevices, at the bottom of the legs, and in any white pores left by the steel wool.

INSTANT AGING. The author leaves the greatest concentration of the black wax in the edges of the cock beading and on the apron below the tabletop overhang. He wipes a thin layer onto the rest of the surfaces.

dissolve the wax and make the finish easy to apply with a brush. If you prefer, you can leave out the black pigment. The gold size acts as a binder to make the pigment adhere to the finish when it dries.

Apply it to corners, crevices, feet, and any light spots. Then rub it with a clean cloth to blend it into the rest of the work-piece. To my eye it gives character and re-creates the soft waxed luster of a piece of furniture that has been taken care of for 250 years.

SEAN CLARKE and his wife, Angela, who helped in the preparation of this article, are the owners of Clarke Co. in Valencia, Calif., specializing in the restoration and refinishing of antiques.

A Short Course in Gilding

Gold has been prized through the ages not only for its luster and color but also for its working properties, one of the most remarkable of which is its ability to be worked as gold leaf. Gold leaf is gold pounded tissue-thin—so thin that if you rub a sheet between your fingers it turns to powder and disappears. Yet, once adhered to a substrate, gold leaf is remarkably strong and durable.

It was in the Renaissance that gold leaf gained widespread use. In houses of the wealthy, in rooms dimly lit by candles and oil lamps, large gilt-framed mirrors gleamed on the walls, their burnished surfaces serving to magnify the light. This brilliant finish was soon adopted by European carvers and furniture makers, and eventually it crossed the Atlantic and gave its name to America's Gilded Age. There is a mystique about gold leafing and a misconception that it is a difficult art. The truth is that while traditional gold leafing like that used on the mirror frame below, known as water gilding, is a finicky, labor-intensive process requiring a dozen or more undercoats of sealer, each one carefully sanded, there is a much simpler

BY
STUART M. ALTSHULER

109

Surface Preparation Is Paramount

In laying gold leaf, surface preparation is critical, because every flaw in the substrate will telegraph through the leaf.

Sanding

SAND FINE AND CLEAN CAREFULLY. After sanding to fine grits, remove dust with a tack cloth. Then use alcohol to clean the surface of any residue from the tack cloth.

Sealing

DON'T AERATE THE BRUSH. It's important to get as smooth a coat of sealer as possible. To avoid getting air bubbles in the finish, remove excess paint by shaking the brush downward instead of wiping it off against the can's lip.

AVOID POOLING AND PUDDLING. After painting on the sealer, go back with a nearly dry brush to clean up any paint that pools in the corners.

Sizing

ADD A SPOT OF COLOR. Sizing is nearly colorless. Adding a drop of Japan color to the sizing makes it easier to see as you brush it on.

START IN THE MIDDLE. To get the thinnest and most even coat of sizing, begin brushing at the middle of a section, then brush out toward both ends.

Laying the Leaf

If the surface has been well prepared, laying the leaf goes with surprising speed. Leaf needn't be applied in any particular order; develop your own technique and rhythm.

SNIP TO SIZE. When working with patent leaf, with its paper backing, use scissors to cut workable pieces.

PLACE THE LEAF. Holding the sheet by the paper backing, keep it taut until it contacts the workpiece.

PRESS INTO PLACE. Then press it into full contact with the workpiece.

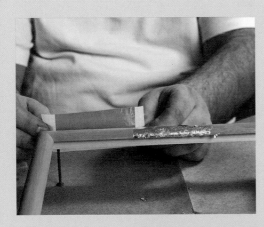

OVERLAP IS EXPECTED. Each sheet of leaf you lay should slightly overlap the previous one.

GET INTO THE CORNERS. Use your finger to get the leaf to conform to inside corners.

BRUSH AWAY THE SEAMS. Using a circular motion, brush off excess leaf with a gold mop. As you do, the seams between sheets of leaf will all but disappear.

SAVE THE SKEWINGS. If you cover your work table with kraft paper, you can crease it and easily pour the excess gold, or skewings, into a jar.

Working With Loose Leaf

Leaf without a paper backing is trickier to work with but offers a wide range of colors and types of leaf not available with backing.

TOO TENDER FOR SCISSORS. Cut loose leaf with gentle pressure from a gilder's knife. To avoid contaminating the gilder's tip (brush), learn to hold it rather than laying it on the bench.

QUICK TIP. After cutting the leaf, lay the gilder's tip against the leaf and draw it away. The leaf should gently adhere to the tip.

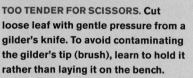

LEAF DELIVERY. Touch the tip to the workpiece, and the gold will cling to the sized surface.

COAXING WITH COTTON. Use a cotton swab to get the gold to conform to the main contours of a carving.

MOP AFTER SWABBING. A gold mop can be used after the cotton swab to press leaf into deep recesses.

approach to applying gold leaf: oil gilding. If you want burnished gold leaf of the highest reflectivity, you must use the water-gilding method (so named because the sizing is water-based). The buildup of coats creates an ideally smooth, slightly resilient surface on which to burnish the gold leaf. But if you can accept less-than-perfect reflectivity, oil gilding is the way to go.

There are four basic steps in the process of oil gilding: sanding, sealing, sizing and laying the gold.

As you prepare a surface for gilding, it is important to note that gold is the least forgiving of all finishes. It will highlight any flaw in the surface to which it is applied. So sand, sand, and sand some more. Gilders refer to 400-grit sandpaper as medium. When you think that your surface is good enough, keep sanding—the results will be quite visible.

Leaf can be applied directly to metal or glass, but a porous material like wood must be sealed before gold is applied. There are several ways to seal wood to accept gold. A traditional method is with a coat of shellac. Fresh shellac is a must; a 1-lb. cut is suffi-cient. Shellac is typically used with a tinted undercoat to ensure that bare wood is not visible when the gold leaf is abraded. For such a treatment, using a coat of Japan color under the shellac works nicely.

Commercial sealer is a simpler alternative to shellac. Most such sealers are available in either yellow ochre or red. The yellow ochre is a particularly good choice for the beginner, because it will hide any small gaps, or holidays, in the gold.

After the sealer comes the adhesive. Traditional oil-based sizing is available in either slow (12-hour) or quick (three-hour) set. Slow-set sizing takes 12 hours to come to tack, but then has 12 hours of open time; quick set takes three hours to come to tack and then has a three-hour working window. Other sizings are available for specialized applications.

Whichever sizing you use, apply the least amount possible. The object is to get a very thin, even coat free of brush strokes. As the sizing comes to tack, it imperceptibly flows out over the surface. The more freely it flows, the less visible your brush strokes will be. I prefer 12-hour sizing, because it flows better and allows you more time to lay the leaf. The sizing is ready for gold when a touch of the finger finds it sticky but leaves no print.

Apply the leaf using the largest pieces you are comfortable working with. Some people lay whole sheets of gold, others find it easier to maneuver small sections. When you have one piece down, lay a second one so that it overlaps the first by ⅛ in. or so. Cover the entire surface with leaf, then go back and fill any small gaps.

Once you've covered the surface and filled any gaps, brush away the excess gold, or skewings, with a gold mop. Hold the brush firmly and use a gentle circular motion. The leaf adheres only to the sizing, not to other leaf, so as you continue to brush over the seams, they will fade, and it will be difficult to tell where each sheet of leaf began and ended.

Some people like to give gold leaf the appearance of an antique. You can create a patina to achieve this effect using caseins—water-soluble, quick-drying flat paints that can be intermixed without muddying. Mix several colors to create a dusty or dirty blend and then apply it with a rag. Rub off some of the mixture, leaving more color, or age, in corners and crevices where dust would naturally fall.

I rarely use a topcoat over gold leaf because it will dull the appearance of the gold. And for surfaces gilded with leaf 22 karat and higher, a topcoat is unnecessary, because they will not tarnish or corrode.

STUART M. ALTSHULER is a contributor to *Fine Woodworking* magazine.

> *There is a mystique about gold leafing and a misconception that it is a difficult art.*

How and Where To Buy Gold Leaf

Gold leaf is sold to craftsmen by the book or by the pack. Each book contains 25 sheets of gold, and you can cover about 2 sq. ft. with a book's worth. A pack contains 20 books.

There are four main types of gold leaf used for gilding. Surface leaf is the traditional leaf used for gilding. Patent leaf, also called transfer leaf, is the same as surface leaf but comes adhered to a thin paper backing, which makes it easier to handle. Glass leaf is similar to surface leaf, but it has fewer imperfections, so it is ideal for signs on glass. Double leaf is like surface leaf but thicker (although not twice as thick); it is useful for gilding objects with sharp edges that might cause thinner leaf to break. All four types come in various shades of gold.

The karat weight of gold—an indicator of the gold's purity, not its weight—is expressed in 24ths. Leaf marked 24K (karat) is pure gold. Leaf marked 23K is 23/24ths gold and 1/24th alloy. Leaf thickness is measured by weighing 1,000 sheets and is expressed in grams. As an example, gold leaf designated 23K, 11g, would be thinner and cost less than 23K, 14g leaf.

Gold leaf costs about $1 a sheet. You can buy gold leaf and gilding supplies from large art stores or from the following companies: Easy Leaf (6001 Santa Monica Blvd., Los Angeles, CA 90038; 800-569-LEAF); Sepp Leaf Products (381 Park Ave. S., Suite 301, New York, NY 10016; 212-683-2840); and Baggot Leaf Co. (430 Broome St., New York, NY 10013; 212-431-4653).

Milk Paint

BY MIKE DUNBAR

Woodworkers have used milk paint since antiquity. It remains a desirable finish today for the same reason it was favored by the ancients and every generation of woodworkers in between. Milk paint is quick, easy, and forgiving. It results in a rich, lustrous, and complex finish that improves with time. Still, it can be applied in an afternoon. Milk paint is not difficult to use, but it is

THIS TRADITIONAL PAINTED FINISH even improves with age.

different from regular paint. And to get the best results, you need to understand those differences.

Milk paint does not chip like regular paint, nor does it produce the boring, perfectly uniform color of modern products. Instead, it has subtle differences of shading that make it much more like the lead- and oil-based paints used in centuries past. As a piece of furniture finished in milk paint ages, worn paint becomes polished and takes on different levels of sheen. The final effect is subtle, lively, and complex. Because of the way this wear plays with light, a milk-paint finish actually gets better as it ages.

Milk paint is nothing more than a mixture of lime, casein, clays, and any one of a variety of earth pigments. In the past, woodworkers mixed their own milk paints using simple formulas handed down from one generation to another. Today, it is far easier to buy it from The Old Fashioned Milk Paint Co. (see Sources on p. 119). The manufacturer offers a palette of 16 different colors.

The paint arrives in powder form and is mixed with water. It has a distinctive smell, but it is not disagreeable. There are no fumes during use, and it can be washed down the kitchen sink when it comes time to clean up. The manufacturer warns that prolonged exposure to lime can burn wet skin and injure eyes. In 25 years of use, I have never experienced either of these problems. I think of the finish as perfectly safe.

What makes milk paint so different from more common products is the fact that milk paint is water based. Oil- and latex-based paints are much thicker than milk paint and sit as a skin on the surface of wood. When struck or scratched, these paints will chip. Being water based, milk paint has far less body and lays on in thinner coats. Also, much of the water-based milk paint soaks into the wood, so it does not chip. In normal use, it will only wear.

Milk paint bonds well only to fresh, raw wood or to itself. I have never had good luck using milk paint over another finish. If a chair has been left unfinished for a long time so that the exposed wood has case-hardened or if areas of the chair are sealed from dirt and oil from human hands, I don't use milk paint.

On the other hand, there are a number of neat tricks available when using milk paint. New colors can be created by mixing the contents of different packages. A favorite finish among chairmakers is to paint a chair with several coats of different colors—the most common sequence being Lexington green, barn red, and pitch black. Over time, the wear caused by repeated use will cut through the various colors, creating a close approximation of the old paint that is so prized by antique collectors. Pitch black over barn red produces a subtle tortoise-shell appearance.

You can also vary the results by changing the amount of water you add. Thinned with one-and-a-half parts water to one part paint, it works well as a colored wash. Thin it even more, and it makes a nice, colored wiping stain. On reproduction pieces made of cherry, I frequently apply a coat of red mixed this way. Brush the mixture onto only one area at a time, let it sit a minute and wipe away the excess with an absorbent cloth.

Milk Paint Choices

A forgiving finish that wears well and long the finish of choice for chairmaker Mike Dunbar, milk paint provides a deep, textured surface to the blanket chest on p. 114. Eighteen years ago, the rocker below was covered in three layers of paint, then left to age with distressed dignity. The signature colors of milk paint (see the Shaker boxes on p. 115) take on a beautiful patina as they age.

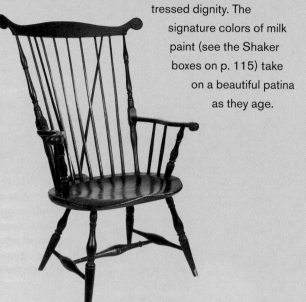

Unfinished Cherry

Lexington Green

Barn Red

Pitch Black

Oiled Finish

AN EASY MIX. For the blanket chest on p. 114, powder and water were mixed in equal amounts. But milk paint can be thinned even more to create a colored wash or wiping stain.

Gearing Up to Paint

As I said, to make milk paint, just add water to the powder. The manufacturer recommends a one-to-one mix. I mix it in a clean, wide-mouthed jar. The wide mouth makes it easier to dip the brush. You can mix the paint with a stirring paddle driven by an electric drill, but I just shake it up like a bartender making a whiskey sour. The action of shaking will result in a paint that is frothy and full of air, like whipped cream. Let it sit for about an hour to allow the air to escape. The solids will settle slowly, so stir it before you start painting and regularly throughout the process.

If you want a smooth surface, strain the paint through an old pair of panty hose or a strainer purchased at a paint supply store. Unstrained milk paint leaves a slightly grainy finish. It is more matte, like an exceedingly fine sand paint.

Once a packet has been opened, the powder will slowly absorb moisture from the air and lose its ability to bond with wood. Therefore, never buy large quantities, only what you need. The unused product will last a lot longer if you seal the bag carefully and store it in a dry environment.

Mixed milk paint also goes bad. It is a good idea to use it only on the day it is mixed. If you are not able to complete the finish in one day, you can stretch the mixed paint's working life by keeping it in the refrigerator. After two days, throw it away.

I generally prepare my project while the froth is settling out of the paint. Milk paint has almost no body and will not fill small holes the way oil or latex will. If your project has any blemishes, fill them with a latex filler, which will accept the paint.

Because milk paint is water based, it will raise the grain of the wood, making it necessary to sand between coats. To save time, raise the grain well before the first coat, using a spray water bottle, available at any hardware store. The trick is to wet the surface thoroughly but not as if you were washing a car. If the water puddles or runs, you are being too liberal.

During the wetting, any glue spills or smears that would prevent the milk paint from bonding will become visible and can be removed with a scraper or pocketknife. Allow the surface to dry completely. Then before applying the first coat of milk paint, finish-sand the wood and dust it with a clean, soft cloth.

The First Coat Seals, and the Second Coat Covers

The manufacturer recommends applying the paint to a wet surface, but I skip this step because of the prewetting and sanding procedure I just outlined. In my experience, the water used to moisten the wood thins the paint so much that a third coat is

EXCESS PAINT TURNS TO DUST AS IT DRIES. A gray Scotch-Brite nylon pad knocks off any rough spots in the second coat.

A CHEAP BRUSH IS ALL YOU NEED. A natural bristle brush– bought for $1 at the local hardware store–is used to apply all coats.

usually required for complete coverage. So you end up doing more work in the long run.

When it comes time to paint, wear an apron to protect your clothes and put down a layer of newspaper or builder's paper to protect your workbench. Milk paint dries quickly and is difficult to remove once it dries.

Milk paint can be applied with a natural bristle brush—the cheap ones with unfinished wood handles and blond bristles. During the first coat, numerous bristles will pull loose and stick in the paint. Flick them

Shake, Spray, and Fill

SHAKEN, NOT STIRRED. In a jar salvaged from the kitchen, the author mixes paint by shaking it as a bartender would mix a drink.

TIME SPENT NOW IS SAVED LATER. Prewetting the wood raises the grain. Sanding leaves a smooth surface ready to absorb paint.

CHOOSE FILLERS CAREFULLY. Milk paint won't adhere to prefinished surfaces, but it will bond to a latex filler.

out with your fingernail. If you miss any, don't worry; they brush away without leaving a blemish when the paint is dry.

Milk paint draws into the wood almost as quickly as it makes contact. This means that you cannot successfully draw it as you can an oil- or latex-based paint. The action is more like daubing. Do not let milk paint puddle on the wood. Brush it vigorously and work it to a thin film so that it spreads and absorbs uniformly.

Fortunately, even if the paint puddles or runs, you still won't have a blemish in most cases. When the paint dries, the thick areas become crusty. Generally, excess dried paint will brush away as a powder. At worst, you may have to break up the crust with your fingernail.

The tendency of milk paint to soak into the wood makes it difficult to cut in—the process of drawing a fine line of paint with a brush. It is not impossible to pick out areas or parts in a different color, but you do have to be careful. If possible, paint different-colored parts separately before assembly.

Milk paint dries through evaporation. This means that on large pieces, some sections will dry before you even get started on others. It's important that you allow the entire piece to dry completely. Drying time is a function of the shop's environment and will take longer on a muggy summer day than in a heated shop in the winter.

The first coat will look like something the cat dragged in. It will be splotchy and uneven. This is no time for a faint heart. If you are trying to achieve a very smooth surface, rub down the first coat with a maroon Scotch-Brite nylon pad. You can use 000 steel wool, but it leaves a lot of steel dust.

Rinse out your brush with running water and store it in a jar of water, so any paint left on the brush doesn't dry. Before applying the second coat, remove excess water from the brush by wiping it over the paper on your workbench.

THINNED LINSEED OIL OVER FLAT PAINT. **A mixture of five parts boiled linseed oil and one part paint thinner is brushed on as a final coat. Excess is wiped away with a lint-free rag.**

Sources

The Old Fashioned Milk Paint Company
436 Main St.
Box 222
Groton, MA 01450-0222
978-448-6336

Because the paint is no longer being absorbed so quickly, the second coat usually covers in less time than the first. This time the paint flows more like an oil- or latex-based product. You still need to spread the paint in a thin, even coat.

As with the first coat, the second coat of milk paint can send the first-time user into fits of panic. The paint dries dead flat—flatter than anything you have ever seen—and you can still see brush overlaps and areas that you touched up. Again, have courage. If you want a very smooth surface, rub the second coat with a gray Scotch-Brite nylon pad. Or rub hard and vigorously with a soft cloth.

Oil Overcoat Holds Everything Down

An oil overcoat has two purposes. First, it pulls the whole finish together and gives it a darker but deeper rich color and luster. Second, it protects the finish from spills that can cause spots on raw milk paint. I mix roughly five parts boiled linseed oil to one part paint thinner. Apply the mixture with a cheap natural bristle brush. Wet all of the painted surfaces on the piece. Overlaps and thin areas in the paint will stand out for several minutes, but they slowly blend to a uniform color. Let the oil stand for about 10 minutes. Then wipe off as much as you can with a soft, lint-free rag. Allow the oil to dry for two days before using the piece.

Some people apply a coat of wax after the oil dries, but I prefer to leave it as it is. The young finish is beautiful but has no character. Character develops with time. Use the piece as you would normally, and enjoy the increasingly subtle and complex finish.

MIKE DUNBAR teaches Windsor chairmaking in Hampton, N.H., and is a contributing editor to *Fine Woodworking* magazine.

Three Finishes for Bird's-Eye Maple

BY TERI MASASCHI

I never would claim that working and finishing bird's-eye maple are easy, but few woods can yield such contrasting appearances. At one end of the spectrum is the natural look, with a clear finish bringing out the wood's three-dimensional quality. In complete contrast is the striking look of antique wood, where a century or more of oxidizing and accumulated patina gives it

Natural

that certain glow and prominent grain. In between, there is the medium-tone appearance, with the eyes highlighted by the finishing process. Using a selection of dyes, stains, glazes, and topcoats, I'll show you how to achieve the appearance of your choice.

The Natural Look, or "Bird's-Eye Lite"

Good surface preparation is especially key to the desired outcome on bird's-eye maple. This wood does have the tendency to tear out during planing. Using a wide-belt sander for larger surfaces and scraping for delicate details, you can eliminate most of the voids. Subsequent sanding with 120-, 150- and 180-grit paper on a random-orbit sander is all that is necessary to prepare the wood for its finish.

Medium

Antique

POP THE FIGURE OF THIS WOOD **using dyes, stains, glazes, and topcoats.**

If you enjoy the clean, crisp look of unstained maple, wood selection is critical: There can be no sapwood, mineral streaks, or widely different colors of stock, because a natural finish can't hide these discrepancies.

For a light finish, use Danish oil or Waterlox Original Sealer thinned with mineral spirits in a one-to-one solution. Pour a liberal amount on the wood and wet-sand with 400-grit paper or a sanding sponge, creating an oil-and-sawdust slurry. This will be driven into the eyes, leaving the surface smooth. One application should be sufficient. Additional coats can be added, but more oil makes the maple more yellow.

The topcoat should be nonyellowing like CAB acrylic lacquer, a pale solvent finish such as Behlen's Water White Restoration Varnish, or a water-based lacquer or urethane. All clear coats should be gloss because the flatteners used to manufacture satin and semigloss coatings dull the wood's appearance. If a lower final sheen is desired, the gloss coat can be rubbed out.

The idea behind this method is that the oil enhances the eyes, while the film coating creates a deeper and more dimensional surface than the oil alone can give.

Bird's-Eye Maple With a Medium Tone

The first step is to apply a tinted wash-coat to the bare wood. This thinned coating, typically dyed dewaxed shellac, adds a layer of color and creates a barrier coat between the bare wood and a layer of glaze.

CREATE A PENETRATING OIL. Mix equal amounts of Danish oil and mineral spirits. To avoid spills when pouring, keep the opening at the top to allow air to enter and liquid to exit smoothly rather than in irregular gulps.

FILL THE EYES AND SMOOTH THE SURFACE. Pour a generous amount of the mixture onto the wood and then sand it in with a 400-grit sanding sponge. The oil-and-sawdust slurry fills voids in the bird's eyes, making them more prominent.

TOPCOAT WITH A CLEAR FINISH. To avoid adding a tone to the natural-looking wood, use a nonyellowing finish, such as Behlen's Water White Restoration Varnish.

Either dissolve some blond shellac flakes or cut Zinsser's SealCoat by 50% with denatured alcohol to form a 1-lb. cut. For each 4 oz. of shellac, add a drop or two (depending on the desired intensity) of a concentrated dye such as TransTint or Wizard Tint. Honey amber or Vandyke brown are beautiful colors on bird's-eye maple. An alternative to tinting the shellac would be to use darker shades of shellac, such as orange or buttonlac. In either case, apply the shellac evenly with a brush or spray gun, let dry, and scuff-sand with 320- or 400-grit paper.

Now apply a second layer of color using a shading and glazing stain. These heavy-bodied pigment glazing stains are designed to go over sealed surfaces only, being too thick and opaque for raw wood. Glazing

stain has enough oil in it to be wiped off a sealed surface easily, leaving only a thin layer of color or glaze. On large surfaces it creates subtle changes in color tones, and if left heavy in corners and profiles, it gives the appearance of built-up patina. I use a warm brown such as Behlen's burnt-umber shading and glazing stain.

After wiping off the surplus, let it dry for at least three hours. Then add another wash-coat of undyed dewaxed blond shellac to set the glaze before topcoating with a solvent- or water-based gloss finish.

Multiple Layers of Color Give an Antique Look

Woodworkers who have built a beautiful period piece with bird's-eye maple face a challenge to re-create the 18th-century tone and, at the same time, pop the figure in a transparent way.

Begin with a coat of water-based honey-amber maple dye. First wet the surfaces with water, and when they're dry, de-whisker them with 220-grit sandpaper on a felt or cork block. This not only eliminates raised grain but also allows greater stain absorption. The dye stain penetrates deep into the wood, creating a perfect tone that will shine through the subsequent layers of color. Wash-coat with a dewaxed dark shellac such as garnet or buttonlac, allow it to dry, and then scuff-sand.

Apply a generous amount of burnt-umber shading and glazing stain, let it sit for a few minutes to bite into the surface, then wipe it off smoothly to leave a thin glaze of color on the surface and more color lodged in any details. Let it dry for three hours and then wash-coat with dewaxed blond shellac to set the glaze. Antique reproductions respond well to this process, which can be repeated to deepen the caramel tone that antiques usually have. After the desired tone has been reached, a second glaze can be added to age the piece. Mix raw-umber shading and glazing liquid with black shading and glazing or Sherwin Williams' Gilsonite (also known as asphaltum), and thin with mineral spirits to a brushing consistency. Apply this mixture over most of the piece and into all of the corners and crevices. Wipe off the bulk of the glaze, leaving dark lines in the deep recesses. This completes the visual perception of antique bird's-eye maple. Seal with a wash-coat of dewaxed shellac and finish with a gloss clear coat.

TERI MASASCHI is a professional finisher, restorer, and instructor who lives near Albuquerque, N.M.

A Medium Tone

COMBINATION DYE AND SEAL. This 2-lb. cut of premixed blond shellac is diluted with an equal volume of denatured alcohol. A few drops of concentrated dye give this wash-coat some color.

FIRST FINISH LAYER. Brush on the dyed shellac. This layer also seals the wood from the next glaze.

A SECOND LAYER OF COLOR. Brush on a shading and glazing stain, then wipe it off. Leave a thin layer of color with a little extra glaze in the corners and voids to give a more interesting look to the piece.

Antique Maple

DYE, THEN SEAL. Apply a water-based dye. When it's dry, seal it with a coat of dark dewaxed shellac, such as buttonlac.

THE FIRST GLAZE. Apply burnt-umber shading and glazing stain to the sanded shellac. Allow it to penetrate, then wipe the surface, leaving residue in any voids.

THE SECOND GLAZE. Mix raw-umber and black shading and glazing stain thinned with mineral spirits.

BRUSH ON THE MIXTURE AND WIPE IT OFF. Residue left in crevices imitates an antique look.

Creating an Antique Painted Finish

I started experimenting with painted finishes that look old because I live in a very old region of the country. The Native American and Spanish Colonial cultures are still very much a part of the look here in New Mexico.

In collaboration with my friend Dwayne Stewart, who's a painter and professional finisher in Kansas City, Mo., I've developed a method that makes even new furniture look like it's been around for a long time.

Selecting and Preparing the Wood

I use old wood whenever I can, but new wood can be stained dark to make it look older.

Tool marks make a big difference, too. I eliminate machine marks with hand tools, and I gouge the wood intentionally. A 17th-century Spanish craftsman here in the desert Southwest might have had an adze, a drawknife, maybe a handplane (but likely

NO, IT WASN'T MADE BY THE CONQUISTADORS. Though it looks like it's been in a Spanish Colonial mission for several hundred years, this hall table is really less than a year old.

An Antique Finish in 12 Steps

1 BURNISH THE EDGES. Furniture doesn't age, or wear, evenly. Sharp corners, edges, and other crisp details soften first. The author uses the shank of a large nail to round over the sharp edges on a tabletop.

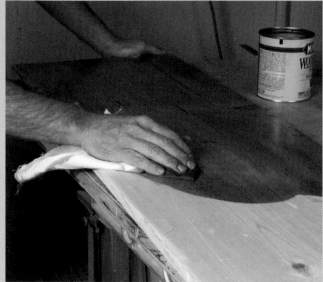

2 FOR A LIGHT WOOD LIKE PINE, USE A DARK STAIN. Because wood changes color as it ages, the author uses a pigmented oil stain (Minwax Early American) to darken this tabletop made of ponderosa pine. But any kind of stain will do. Then he lets the stain dry according to the manufacturer's instructions.

3 SEAL IN THE COLOR WITH A CLEAR COAT. The author brushes on two coats of lacquer, but other clear finishes will work as well. Just be sure to use something with a low sheen.

4 SCUFF-SAND THE CLEAR COAT. A quick once-over with 220-grit dulls the sheen and gives the clear coat enough tooth to hold a coat of paint.

5 WAX PREVENTS PAINT FROM ADHERING, which lets the stained wood show through. Rub a bar of paraffin lightly over the edge and a bit on the top. Let the bar skip along, so the pattern will be uneven. Wax the edge more heavily, but still intermittently.

6 APPLY A FIRST COAT OF FLAT LATEX PAINT. Coverage doesn't have to be perfectly even, and it's probably better that way. Choose a color that contrasts well with the topcoat. Give it an hour or two (or whatever it says on the can) to dry.

7 BRUSH ON A COAT OF HIDE GLUE. The author uses premixed liquid hide glue, but hot hide glue also works. If the premixed glue appears too thick to brush out, thin it slightly with some warm water. Mix well before applying it. A thicker coat will give you fewer, bigger cracks in the next layer of paint; a thinner coat will give you smaller cracks but more of them. Don't worry about laying down an even coat (variations in the size of the cracks look more realistic), but apply the glue in only one direction. If you're haphazard with your strokes, the crackle pattern won't look right. This is the only step you really have to be finicky about. Give the glue half an hour or so to dry.

8 APPLY A SECOND COAT OF FLAT LATEX. Make sure that the paint is flat; semigloss or gloss paint won't crackle. Keep a wet edge, move quickly and don't go over your previous strokes, or you'll fill in the cracks. This second coat starts to crackle almost immediately. Let it dry thoroughly, preferably overnight.

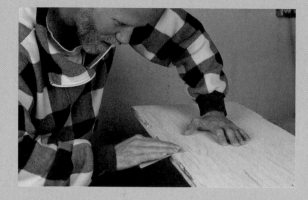

9&10 SCRAPE AND THEN SAND THE TOP AND EDGES. When the second coat of paint is dry, use a paint scraper to remove paint sitting on top of the wax. The scraper also will dislodge loose chunks of paint to reveal the first layer below. Mist the surface with water, and then rub with your fingers to create an even more authentic look. Sand lightly to soften sharp edges.

11 APPLY A COAT OF MEDIUM- OR DARK-TINTED LIQUID WAX. The author uses Watco dark-satin finishing wax. This wax seeps into all the cracks and recesses and gives the whole piece a darker, almost dirty look–instant patina. Temperature affects drying time. The author usually waits about 10 to 15 minutes.

12 REMOVE MOST OF THE TINTED WAX WITH A CLEAN RAG. If the whole piece or just some areas are too dark, you can remove some of the color. Apply a clear coat of paste wax and rub vigorously. The solvent in the wax lifts the excess color from the surface. The paste wax protects the surface, too.

not) and not much more. And he certainly didn't have any fancy sharpening stones. So the surfaces you see on most old furniture around here is kind of rough. I achieve a similar effect by planing against the grain in places (especially near knots), causing tearout, skewing the blade on my plane so it gouges the surface, keeping the blade intentionally dull and burnishing sharp edges. This may run counter to everything you've learned, but the results are convincing (see the photo on p. 125).

Once I'm happy with the surface, finishing begins. Because I use latex paint and a quick-drying clear coat, I can complete the process in less than two days (see the sidebar on pp. 126–128). Not bad for a finish that looks like it's seen some history.

KIRT KIRKPATRICK lives in Albuquerque, N.M. He carves and builds furniture and doors.

Finishing Mahogany

BY JEFF JEWITT

When the cabinetmakers in England and America who built early 18th-century furniture fell in love with mahogany, most of the wood was of a color and quality that few woodworkers will have the chance to work with ever again. Those old-growth trees of Cuban and Santo Domingan mahogany (Swietenia mahagoni) yielded lumber with a much darker color and a finer texture than what's commonly available now. I first saw that wood up close many years ago, when I toured the collection of American furniture at a museum in Williamsburg, Va. The first thing that struck me was the color of those pieces: It wasn't just the patina—it was simply awe-inspiring wood. So when I recently had the chance to put a finish on a piecrust table made with a single-plank top, I knew I had to come up with a way to coax that rich, dark finish from the lighter color of the Central and South American (also called Honduras) mahogany (S. macrophylla) available today.

TRANSFORM THE LIGHT-PINK color of freshly milled mahogany into the deep, rich shades of old-world furniture.

Step 1: Start With a Water-Based Dye Stain

An amber-colored stain as the first coat of color does two things: It gives the lumber an aged look, and it evens out different shades inherent in the wood.

RAISE THE GRAIN BEFORE THE FIRST COAT. Before applying a water-based dye stain, wet the surface thoroughly to raise the grain, then let it dry. Sand down the raised fibers before applying the dye stain. The result is a smoother finish than you'd get without taking this preliminary step.

SPRAY IT ON FOR EVEN COVERAGE. An inexpensive plastic spray bottle is a great tool for applying water-based dye stain quickly and evenly.

Lay on the First Layer of Color

It is not uncommon to find worm holes in otherwise perfectly sound mahogany lumber. To avoid wasting a lot of wood, you can fill and color them easily (see the sidebar on p. 133). After that, you can lay on the first level of color. I use an amber-colored water-soluble dye as a base coat to mimic an old finish. The amber undertone evens out color variations in the wood and adds depth to the final finish. I prefer water-soluble dyes because they're easier to control. Also, they tend to absorb more evenly into the wood than alcohol-based dye stains, which dry faster and leave behind unsightly lap marks.

Before applying the stain, sand the piece with 220-grit paper, then raise the grain by wiping the surface with distilled water to minimize any further grain-raising. (Tap water can contain mineral impurities that may discolor the wood.) Wait several hours for the water to dry, then resand with the 220-grit paper.

Use a plant mister to spray on the amber dye, saturating the surface quickly and thoroughly. Water-based dyes are very forgiving compared with alcohol-based dyes, but make sure you soak up any excess with clean rags. After the amber dye has dried, scuff the dry surface using a gray synthetic abrasive pad such as Scotch-Brite brand; go lightly so that you don't cut through the dye.

Mix the Second Color Into an Oil-Sealer Coat

Now it's time to add the second, primary overtone of color. With this table, I used a technique that I first heard about from Rob Millard, who builds reproductions of 18th-century furniture. To get an aged effect and a rich color, use boiled linseed oil colored with dye. You can use an oil-soluble dry powder or a liquid concentrate like I used on this table (see Sources on p. 135). Practice on some scraps first to get the effect you want. To enrich the yellow undertone of the first color, I used equal amounts of TransTint brown mahogany and reddish-brown liquid dyes, mixing 5 ml of each into 100 ml of boiled linseed oil.

Mix the color into the oil in precise amounts and keep a record so that you can duplicate the mixture if you run out. Apply the oil by vigorously wiping it on with a rag in a circular motion; you can use a small brush for intricate shapes. Don't add thinners to the oil because it causes dark circles to form around the pores where the color becomes too concentrated. If the piece becomes too dark, just wipe the colored oil with a new coat of clear oil or a rag dampened with alcohol to remove some of the color.

ABRASIVE PADS CONFORM TO TIGHT SPACES. **To smooth out intricate shapes after staining, abrasive pads work better than sandpaper, and they last longer.**

Fill the Grain With a Rottenstone Slurry

As an option, you can fill the grain in the tabletop at this stage, rather than waiting for the oil to dry and using a paste wood filler. Filled grain results in a smoother surface after the topcoats have been applied. Or you can leave it unfilled. My preference for tabletops is for a filled surface, so I added some more clear oil, sprinkled some rottenstone on the surface and padded the slurry mixture into the grain of the wood with a circular motion. The rottenstone isn't as abrasive as pumice, which might cut through the dye and the undertone color. Also, the gray rottenstone adds a bit of darker color when it's mixed with the oil. After the rottenstone filler has set up for several hours, use a wadded clean cloth to wipe off any excess slurry remaining on the surface. Let that last coat of oil dry for at

Step 2: Seal the Wood With a Coat of Tinted Oil

ELBOW GREASE APPRECIATED HERE. Saturate a wiping rag with the dyed-oil mixture and apply it quickly and efficiently, wiping in a circular motion.

Powdered or liquid dyes mixed with oil will stain and seal the wood in one step. The author uses boiled linseed oil. Be precise and keep track of the amounts that you mix so that you can duplicate the same concentration if you run out.

USE A BRUSH TO DO WHAT THE RAG COULDN'T. The dampened rag may not effectively stain detailed areas, such as the carved edge of this table.

EVEN OUT THE COLOR. After applying the first coat of tinted oil, a rag dampened with alcohol or a new coat of clear oil will help even out the color. The alcohol will dilute the dye without affecting the oil sealer.

least three days. If it's cool (65°F or less) and damp in your shop, let the coat dry for a week.

Build up the Topcoats in Thin Layers

You can choose from a wide range of topcoats—a solvent-based wiping varnish, spray lacquer or even water-based finishes if you apply dewaxed shellac first—as a barrier coat over the oil. For this job, I opted for the classic and traditional shellac finish. For brushing shellac, I prefer a 1½-lb. cut. Because a gallon of shellac was much more than I needed, I just factored the ratio down to 3 oz. of shellac flakes mixed into a pint of alcohol.

I really like the subtleties of texture you get with a brushed-on shellac finish. I use a technique I learned from Don Williams at the Smithsonian Institution many years ago. The trick is to apply the fast-drying shellac in whisper-thin strokes with a very finely bristled synthetic brush, such as the Taklon brushes sold in specialty catalogs and art supply stores. For this table I used two widths—a 2-in. brush for the flat top and a 1-in. brush for the intricately carved base.

Filling the Inevitable Worm Holes

In most extrawide mahogany boards, you'll often find large worm holes near the edges. You can cut them out, but then you risk losing your chance to make a one-piece top, and you waste a lot of lumber. I've used all sorts of putties and fillers, and I've come to the conclusion  that the best solution is to use a nonshrinking auto-body filler, such as Bondo brand. I've used Bondo for 20 years now in repair work, and while I suspect that some purists may despise it, the product has several things going for it.

First, it's absolutely nonshrinking, so after two or three years, you won't notice any depression where the hole was. Second, the color of the mixed putty is a pinkish red that matches the natural color of the mahogany, and it's easy to tweak to get the final color of the finish. When you apply Bondo to an open-grain wood such as mahogany, it's important to apply masking tape around the hole so that you don't get any Bondo in the grain, which will show up later in the finishing process. Let the Bondo dry several hours, then remove the tape and sand the surface level. After the subsequent staining and first coat of shellac finish, you can further refine the putty with some dry pigment colors mixed with shellac, if necessary.

MIX DRY PIGMENTS INTO A LITTLE SHELLAC. After doing this a few times, you really can develop an artist's eye for color.

PAINT AROUND THE RIM OF THE FILLED HOLE. The distinct black line left around the rim needs to be covered with a nearly opaque coating of color.

ADD SOME FAUX GRAIN. Small, darker-tinted lines will look like grain texture after a finish goes on over the repair.

TWEAK THE COLOR AFTER THE STAIN HAS BEEN APPLIED. After the sealer coat of oil goes on but before the topcoat, tweak the final color of the repaired area.

Step 3: Build up the Finish With Thin Coats

The author chose seedlac shellac for the finish on this table because it adds more color to the surface and dries quickly, so he can apply three thin coats in a day. Shellac also bonds well to a surface that was sealed with linseed oil.

SMALL BRUSHES ARE BETTER FOR TIGHT SPACES. Slap on several thin coats with a small brush to avoid muddling up carving details.

DEWAX YOUR OWN SHELLAC. Mix shellac several days ahead of time to allow impurities to settle out of the mixture. Skim the clear shellac off the top with a syringe.

WORK TOWARD THE CENTER. Lay down each brush stroke of thin shellac quickly. Brush from the outside edge toward the center of the table to keep the finish from pooling at the shaped edge.

A single 1½-in. brush would suffice if you don't want to buy both sizes (these brushes are rather pricey).

To apply, dip the brush about halfway into the shellac solution. With shellac, bubbles aren't a problem like they are with brushing varnish, so you can scrape off the excess shellac by dragging the bristles across the lip of the jar. The raised, molded edge of this table can be a challenge for laying on a finish, but this brush excels at the task. Because it doesn't hold a great deal of finish (like a larger brush with an internal reservoir would), this small brush doesn't deposit a pool of shellac when it first touches the surface. And because it has a finely chiseled edge, you can place the brush down lightly right where the edge of the raised molding meets the flat surface of the tabletop and drag it gently toward the center. Use minimal pressure and leave just a whisper-thin film of shellac. When you start to run out, dunk the brush into the shellac again and feather each new stroke into where you left off with the last one. Brushing shellac this way takes a bit of practice, so start on the undersides of a project to get the feel for it. For the intricately carved parts, I use a slapping or flicking motion to apply the shellac. The fast-drying nature of shellac keeps dust pimples from forming in the finish, and you can keep building up new coats very quickly.

I usually build up at least three coats in a day, let it dry overnight and then lightly sand the surface with 600-grit wet-or-dry sandpaper for the flat areas and gray synthetic pads for the complex shapes. Once the shellac has dried for at least three days, you can dull the surface with 0000 steel wool if you want more of a matte sheen. Because all of the layers of shellac melt into one another as the last one dries, there's little danger of rubbing through the finish. If you have to remove some brush marks, use 600-grit sandpaper first, and then follow that with the 0000 steel wool. A light coat of paste wax will bring up a dull surface to a satiny sheen.

JEFF JEWITT is a contributing editor of *Fine Woodworking* magazine and the author of *Taunton's Complete Illustrated Guide to Finishing*.

Sources

J.E. Moser's powdered dyes, Wizard Tints liquid dyes, and rottenstone:

Woodworker's Supply
800-645-9292
www.woodworker.com

TransTint liquid dyes and rottenstone:

Woodcraft
800-225-1153
www.woodcraft.com

Fill the Grain for a Smooth Top

Fill only the top surface of the tabletop. A second, fresh coat of oil mixed with some rottenstone sprinkled over the surface forms a slurry of paste that fills the open grain, leaving a smoother finish after topcoats are applied over it. This step is not recommended for intricately carved details, like those on the table legs.

SPRINKLE IT ON AND RUB IT IN. Swabbed in a circular motion, the rottenstone and oil form a gray-colored slurry that fills the open grain on the tabletop.

Making Wood Look Old

BY JEFF JEWITT

From a magnificent specimen of Cuban mahogany to a humble piece of white pine, wood looks better as it ages. All woods mature with use and time, developing the patina so valued in antique furniture. In my conservation and restoration business, I need to match the look of old wood to new when I'm fabricating missing parts for antique furniture.

I try to simulate the order in which the wear and tear would have happened naturally. I start by matching the surface texture of the new wood with the old. I follow that with a dye stain, distress marks and glazing coats to add more color. Then I apply a finish to match the original.

Match the Original Surface Texture First

Furnituremakers of two centuries ago prepared wood differently from the way we do it now. Lumber was dressed, shaped and made ready for finishing solely by hand. Their tools left distinctive marks on the

BY ADDING TEXTURE, DYE STAINS, AND GLAZES, **even lumberyard pine can be transformed.**

wood very different from those left by modern milling and sanding methods. Edges and moldings were shaped with molding planes or carved with gouges and chisels. After planing, surfaces that would show were smoothed and evened out with scrapers or glass paper (made by pulverizing glass and sifting it over glue-sized parchment).

Even on some very fine, more formal antique furniture, you'll often find marks from tools such as rasps and files that were used to clean up the ridges left by saw-blades and chisels. Molding planes produced crisp, deep profiles unattainable with many modern shaping bits. Although results may seem somewhat crude by today's standards, the goal then was the same as it is now—to produce as flawless a surface as possible.

Flat surfaces on many country-style antiques have a slightly scalloped appearance produced by fore planes, or scrub planes, and scrapers. The scallops are readily apparent under a finish and when viewed in backlighting. To re-create this effect, I ground a very slight convex profile on the blade of an old jack plane (see the photo at right), making sure to relieve the corners of the blade. A very small relief is all that's necessary. Flexing a scraper with your fingers will create a similar pattern. When you use any of these tools, small tearouts or other imperfections in the wood—a sign of handwork—should be left alone.

Patina is More than an Old Finish

Patina is the surface appearance of something that has grown beautiful with age or use. The much desired patina on antique furniture involves alteration of both the surface color and the texture of the piece as it ages.

Wood contains natural dyes and pigments responsible for the characteristic color of each species. A change in color, a result of exposure to light and air (photo-oxidation),

Match the Tool Marks

PERIOD TOOLS MATCH THE SURFACE TEXTURE. Handplaning with a re-ground blade in an old jack plane produces the same pattern left by a scrub plane on the original hutch.

may be the most obvious effect of age. As a rule, light-colored woods darken, and dark-colored woods lighten.

Another kind of patina develops as stains and finishes age and as wax builds up on the surface of the wood. Photo-oxidation causes dyes and pigments to fade and finishes to yellow and darken. Over the years, polishes and waxes build up in corners, cracks and crevices and act as a magnet for dust, which accumulates on surfaces that are not regularly cleaned.

Most old furniture ends up soiled, dented, scratched, eaten by insects or worn-out from normal use and handling. Oils from skin produce a grimy buildup around hardware and other areas where furniture is handled. The bottoms of legs get banged up the most. Sharp edges and corners that are regularly handled become rounded. Everyday contact with clothes and shoes will eventually wear finishes and stains down to bare wood.

Re-Create the Patina

FOUR HOURS IN THE SUN show a dramatic color change in this piece of cherry. The center of the board was covered with duct tape to keep the light out, and the right half was coated with thinner to approximate a clear finish.

TEST THE STAIN ON SCRAP FIRST. The author used a cutoff from the new pine shelf to fine-tune his custom-mixed dye. By adding small amounts of red dye to his initial mix, he was able to get a better match.

Use dyes, bleach, and light to change the color of wood You can duplicate the effect of light on wood with either dyes or chemicals. Both produce a color change within the structure of the wood. Although their effects are similar, one very subtle difference is that dyes tend to accentuate figure and grain and chemicals do not. Dyes are, by far, easier and safer to use. They can

be soluble in alcohol or water. Some alcohol dyes are extremely light-sensitive, and they will not hold their color over time. Water-based dyes tend to be less vivid than alcohol dyes and produce a more believable color. Although water-based dyes raise the grain in wood, producing a rough texture, the problem can be minimized by applying a wash coat of plain water and sanding off the fuzz after the surface dries before the dye goes on.

In almost all light-colored species, a yellowish-brown dye stain will simulate the color of aged wood. This stain color is sold premixed by many companies, often called honey or amber, but you can make your own from powdered dyes in primary colors. The formula I use most is 10 parts lemon yellow, one part red, and one part black by weight, not volume. Use this color on birch, maple, and oak. It also works well for warming up the cold tones of kiln-dried walnut. Used on Honduras mahogany, it will kill the pink tone in preparation for subsequent coloring layers. With one or two more parts of red added, a nice aged pine color is the result (see the bottom photo at left).

Some dark woods—rosewood, teak, walnut, and old Cuban mahogany—lighten considerably after being exposed to light for a long time. To match these woods, you may need to bleach the new wood first and then treat it with a dye stain.

Use a two-part bleach of sodium hydroxide and hydrogen peroxide. Avoid using any other chemicals on woods that have been bleached: A chemical reaction may create harmful fumes.

Some woods, such as poplar and cherry, darken considerably after only limited exposure to sunlight (see the upper photo at left). Cherry will darken in ambient room light after a few years to a dark, reddish orange. To hasten this process, finish it with a light coat of boiled linseed oil followed by the finish of your choice. After several months, you will have a color that would normally take longer to achieve.

Distressing: when and how to alter the surface You can imitate dents by using the tang of a file after the first coat of stain but before the glaze goes on. Scratches can be made with a piece of glass or a wire brush (see the top photo at right). Very small drill bits and the point of an awl will mimic damage done by worms (see the bottom photos at right). Drill the wormholes after the finish has been applied but before the last coat of tinted wax.

To wear away edges, wrap some thick twine or thin rope around your fingers, and pull it back and forth, shoe-shine style, across the edges of tops and stretchers. To round off corners, use a brick, and then burnish the wood smooth with a piece of hard maple. Anything goes, except overdoing it. Too much wear will look contrived.

Finish the Job with a Glaze

The best way to duplicate the depth of color in old wood is with a glaze. Glazes are thin, transparent layers of color applied over another color. Before applying a glaze, it is best to seal in the first layer of color with one or two coats of finish. I prefer shellac. To match most old furniture, the best glazing colors are brown, umber and sienna—sometimes called earth colors. You can use a premixed glaze, or you can make your own if you want better control over the color.

I prefer to use a clear glaze medium (like Behlen's heavy-bodied glazing stain, which is thick and has a long open time). I tint the glaze with dry pigments. Unlike dyes that dissolve into water or alcohol, pigments are suspended in the glaze medium. I also tint with Japan colors, a kind of concentrated paint that will mix easily with oil-based products.

Normally, I do all the distressing before I apply the glaze because the glaze will collect in dents and scratches and provide a very convincing effect. I brush the glaze over the entire piece (see the top left photo

Add Some Wear and Tear

WIRE BRUSHES ABRADE THE SURFACE and mimic the wear and tear of two centuries of use. Glass can also be used to make similar scars.

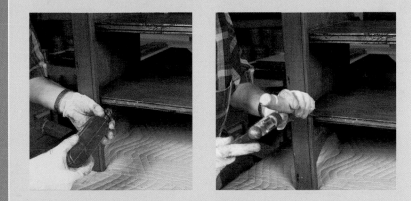

COUNTERFEIT WORMHOLES. After applying a shellac finish but before the final coat of dark, tinted wax, the author uses a small drill bit and the point of an awl to match damage done by worms.

on p. 140) to add an overall color effect or selectively dab it in crevices and corners where wax is likely to build up (see the middle photo on p. 140). The oils in glaze mediums never dry fully, so it's normal to feel some tackiness, even after several days. Glazes and dry pigments are available in many woodworking supply catalogs. Japan colors can be found at professional finishing suppliers or at some paint stores.

Glazes should be sealed with at least one coat of clear finish. It's best to spray on shellac or lacquer. If you have to use a brush, flow on a thin, 1-lb. cut of shellac

Apply a Glaze To Add Depth

A GLAZE ADDS DEPTH AND COLOR. After applying a glaze with a brush, the author controls the amount of color left on the surface as he wipes it off with a clean rag. When he highlights some areas more than others, he dabs on the glaze selectively and blends it in with a dry brush. This technique will also add extra color to distress marks.

FINAL ADJUSTMENTS BEFORE THE FINISH GOES ON. The author wedge-fit the new shelf into this antique dry sink and added another coat of glaze to adjust the color. When the color was right, he removed the shelf and applied a sealer coat of shellac.

without applying too much pressure. You can follow that with a varnish. The sealcoat of shellac is important because the varnish may not bond well to the glaze.

As a final step, I rub it out with steel wool and a dark wax, such as Liberon or Behlen's brown wax. My favorite is Antiquax brown wax. It's tinted with oil-soluble dyes and pigments and matches the look of built-up old wax beautifully. I apply the wax by unraveling a piece of 0000 steel wool and refolding it into quarters. I squirt some mineral spirits onto the pad, dip it into the can of wax and smear it all over the wood surface, working the wax into corners and distress marks. After the wax hazes over, I buff the surface with a clean cloth.

JEFF JEWITT is a contributing editor to *Fine Woodworking* magazine and the author of *Taunton's Complete Illustrated Guide to Finishing*.

Repairing a Worn Finish Without Refinishing

As a restorer, primarily of 20th-century furniture, one of my typical problems is how to improve an existing finish for a customer who is not ready to have the furniture stripped and refinished. More often than not, the furniture doesn't really need such drastic measures.

In cases like that, I've found alcohol-soluble dyes to be the most effective solution among the options available. These dyes receive mostly peripheral treatment in discussions about coloring wood. They are vastly more difficult to apply than oil-based pigment stains, and many of them are not

as lightfast as water-soluble anilines. Yet when it comes to touching up existing finishes, I regard alcohol-soluble dyes as the premier colorant. Their capacity to bite into a finish or sealed wood makes them uniquely suited for restoring worn finishes (see the top left photo on p. 142).

Only Your Chemist Knows for Sure ...

Two kinds of alcohol-soluble dyes are commonly available: basic dyes and metal-complex dyes. Both may be sold as aniline dyes (see the sidebar on p. 143). Basic dyes,

BY
PINCHAS WASSERMAN

NO STRIPPING REQUIRED. **Working with alcohol-soluble dyes and a fine brush, the author makes repairs to this walnut desk that will be virtually undetectable.**

PADDING LACQUER APPLIED BY CLOTH. **Applied with a quick, buffing motion, padding lacquer blends finish repairs and seals in alcohol-soluble dyes.**

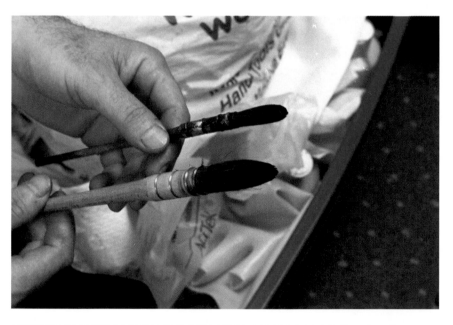

SQUIRREL-HAIR BRUSHES FOR BLENDING LARGE AREAS OF COLOR. **Keep brushes soft and supple with occasional dips in denatured alcohol.**

available through many woodworking catalogs, are the most common and are available in a greater range of premixed wood-tone colors. Not all of these are considered light-fast. But with small areas of worn or chipped finishes, lightfastness is not that important.

Metal-complex dyes, which are manufactured by Ciba-Geigy and BASF (see Sources on the facing page), are less common, more expensive (not that you'll need much for touch-up work) and more resistant to fading. For practical purposes when touching up finishes, there is not a great difference between the two. Both are excellent, powerful dyes.

Small Amounts of Alcohol and Shellac

After mixing dyes with denatured alcohol, I combine the solution with a finish resin. I prefer shellac because it is less toxic and easier to manipulate than lacquer. If I make a mistake when applying the finish, it's relatively easy to remove with alcohol, provided

Sources

The first two companies on this list are manufacturers, and the rest are suppliers of dyes and/or brushes.

BASF
Mount Olive, N.J.
800-669-2273

Ciba-Geigy
Newport, Del.
302-992-5600

Homestead Finishing Products
Cleveland, Ohio
440-582-8929

Liberon/Star Supplies
Mendocino, Calif.
800-245-5611

Olde Mill Cabinet Shoppe
York, Pa.
717-755-8884

Pearl Paint Co.
New York, N.Y.
800-451-7327

W.D. Lockwood Co.
New York, N.Y.
212-966-4046

the dyes are used on top of the finish and not on raw wood. The denatured alcohol in the finish may damage the surrounding surface, but that is easily repaired by applying padding lacquer and rapidly buffing the surface with a lint-free rag (see the top right photo on the facing page). Alcohol-soluble dyes also can be used to tint lacquer, which is a good choice if the repair area is large. I've had good luck with a brushing lacquer such as Deft's clear gloss. It dries relatively slowly.

Typically, I often use less resin for the initial coloring, then topcoat with a greater proportion of resin. First I dissolve the dye in pure alcohol, and then I add shellac in small amounts. I use mostly super blond shellac that I mix from dry flakes. It seems to work on both light and dark finishes. Zinsser's premixed clear shellac (available in most hardware stores) is a less expensive substitute, and its water and wax content is not a factor in touch-up work. Buttonlac, less refined than orange or blond shellac, is good for dark finishes and adds a little opacity to a dye. Alcohol dyes are transparent.

If you need true opacity in a stain, you must turn to pigment powders, Japan colors, or glazing stains to do the job.

I apply alcohol dyes in one of four ways: with a brush, a padding cloth, felt, or an airbrush. Pointed red sable brushes, no. 2 and no. 4, are my most-used brushes for fine detail work. For larger areas, I use squirrel-hair polisher's mops, no. 4 and no. 8, the smaller being the more useful (see the bottom photo on the facing page).

To match an existing finish, orange and blue-black dyes will suffice to create many of the common furniture browns. The steady addition of small amounts of black will lead you through maple browns to walnut. Often, the addition of yellow or red will swing the color one way or another. Try out your dye and shellac mix on a small area, and topcoat it to see how it will look. The topcoat will make the color look bolder and darker.

PINCHAS WASSERMAN often travels to clients' homes to restore furniture. He lives in Lakewood, N.J.

Burning In
Invisible Repairs

BY ROBERT JUDD

BLENDING SEVERAL COLORS ON a hot knife yields just the right shade for an invisible repair. After mixing the resin thoroughly with a small screwdriver, the author flows the molten resin into the damaged area. Burn-in repairs will accept virtually any topcoat.

Whether trying to rescue a hand-polished antique or save a chunk of exotic hardwood from the scrap pile, burn-in sticks and a hot knife can make virtually invisible repairs. A distant cousin of sealing wax, burn-in techniques have been around for centuries. Burning-in can disguise or cosmetically cover scratches, chips, and other damage in a finely finished piece. The repair sticks are available in a host of colors and tints and readily intermix to match any color. Because the various resins and materials used to formulate the repair sticks accept virtually any topcoat, the repair's finish can precisely match the original. A burn-in repair is a reversible process; you can scrape it out and start over if you don't like the color match or result. These simple repairs can save hours of rebuilding or refinishing time.

In this chapter, I'll look at the burn-in repair process: color matching, preparation, filling the defect, leveling the repair, adding wood-grain details, and touch-up finishing. Before trying to repair your favorite piece of furniture, I suggest practicing on a scrap panel of finished wood. It's a simple process, and the basic skills can be learned in a couple of hours. But you also can spend a lifetime perfecting those skills. If you're dealing with a valuable antique, you should consult a professional prior to attempting any repair.

Tools and Materials

Burn-in repairs don't require a huge inventory of expensive tools, compressors, and spray guns. A hot knife, a selection of shellac-resin sticks, a few other miscellaneous supplies and a can of spray lacquer can get you through most of the repairs that you'll encounter (see Sources on p. 149).

The sticks are melted into place using a hot knife, either a thermostatically controlled electric knife or a manual knife with an alcohol lamp using denatured alcohol as its fuel. Don't try to use a candle as a heat source because it produces soot that mixes with and changes the color of the repair material. I've also heard of using soldering irons, but I don't advocate the practice. The iron is too hot and can burn the stick shellac, as well as the wood you are trying to repair.

I prefer the electric knife because it poses little fire hazard, and it maintains a consistent temperature. My tool of choice is a lightweight, slim, and highly maneuverable knife made by Hot Tools, Inc. (see Sources on p. 149). But I also carry an alcohol lamp in my tool kit for those occasions when no electricity or lack of room makes a manual knife a logical choice.

The shellac-resin sticks are available in a wide variety of colors and tints. And different colors can be melted and mixed together on the hot knife to make the exact shade necessary for a perfect match. Some colors

PLACING SHELLAC-RESIN sticks directly on the piece to be repaired is the best way to get a sense of the color match. This technique also helps in selecting the shades that need to be blended, such as the three different colored sticks shown here.

are available translucent or opaque, which can help make certain repairs far less noticeable. The translucent shades are perfect for repairs when just the finish is damaged and not the underlying wood. This situation is identified by no telltale color changes in the damaged area. A color change indicates broken wood fibers that will require opaque colors. But opaque and translucent colors can be intermixed to suit any repair situation.

Other than the new Concept 2000 repair system by Mohawk (see Sources on p. 149 and the sidebar on p. 147), shellac resins are very brittle when cool and can chip when used on corners or other areas subject to sharp impact. The resin has no strength to hold nails or screws, so it should be used for only cosmetic repairs.

Color-Matching

Probably the most important step involved in making a good repair is color matching. It is an art that takes some practice, but color matching can be learned. Most wood has a background shade that is dominant in creating the impression of color. Quickly glance at a piece that needs repair. The color you see in that quick look is the one that you want to match. Now look closely at the piece. You will immediately notice that it is made up of many colors that are subtly blended.

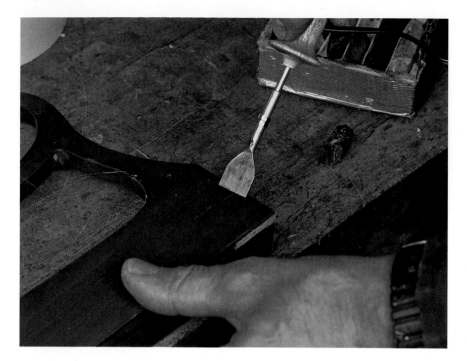

SMOOTH THE REPAIR WITH THE HOT KNIFE by drawing the knife over the resin and then wiping the excess resin from the knife. Keep the knife moving because it is easy to burn the surrounding finish.

By carefully selecting the right shades of resin sticks, repairs also can be subtly blended.

As a general rule on medium and dark finishes, if you can't get an exact match, it is better to make your repair darker than the surrounding wood. With lighter woods, it is better to err on the lighter side. This will help prevent high contrast situations, which stand out and call attention to your repairs.

A trick that helps me match colors is to place some sticks on the piece to be repaired, as shown in the photo on p. 145. Looking at the color in situ is the best way of knowing if a single stick will make a good match.

Because there are so many formulas and proprietary resins used, the manufacturers' color names can be a bit confusing. Each manufacturer has its own idea of what color "antique mahogany" or "golden oak" should be. The key is to match the wood to the repair stick color, not the name. It's all right to use a dark walnut to repair a piece of mahogany if the color match is good.

Often you will need to mix or blend colors on the knife while the resin is in a liquid state, as shown in the photo on p. 144. As a rule of thumb, if you are mixing more

than three colors, you are probably in trouble; just wipe the knife clean on a rag and start again.

By purchasing a set of sticks, you will have a better chance of having the right colors on hand. I recommend buying a set of small, 2-in.-long sticks because you can get a great selection for a modest price. Even though 2 in. is the smallest size, the sticks will still go a long way because so little material is used for each repair.

Making the Repair

Before starting a repair, the first step is to clean the damaged area using a rag dampened with VM&P (Varnish Makers and Painters) naphtha. This solvent will remove wax and dry in a matter of minutes, leaving a powdery residue that can be wiped off with a clean cloth. I then apply Burn-In Balm (Mohawk) or Patch Lube (Star) around the damaged areas. These thick ointments, the consistency of Vaseline petroleum jelly, act as heat sinks and help prevent burning the surrounding finish. They also act as repellents, so the resin adheres only in the damaged areas. A small bottle lasts a long, long time and makes repairs easier and neater.

Before beginning the repair, clean the knife to avoid any color contamination from residue clinging to the blade. Preheat an electric knife three to five minutes or a manual knife 30 seconds, and wipe it clean with a rag or scrape it clean with a single-edge razor blade. When you apply the knife to the stick, the resin should flow smoothly rather than bubble or boil, a clear sign the knife's too hot. After melting enough material to slightly overfill the damage, allow the molten resin to flow into the damaged area, creating a slight dome of excess material.

Wipe the knife clean, and then smooth the repair by drawing the knife over the resin, always working toward you, as shown in the photo on p. 148. Repeat the process of wiping the knife clean and stroking the

Burning-In for Beginners

As I was putting together the information on burn-in repairs, my Mohawk finishing products salesman introduced me to Concept 2000, a new repair system that was recently introduced. After working with Concept 2000, I found the system eliminates or minimizes many of the common problem areas, especially for the novice. The repair sticks are flexible, so repairs made with the new sticks won't be as fragile as the brittle traditional sticks. And the halo effect, a glossy ring left by traditional burn-in repairs, is gone because the sticks dry flat, making it easier to blend in the repairs.

Lower Temperatures for Better Results

What really sets the Concept 2000 system apart from the traditional method is the fact that the burn-in knife is cooler than the old-style knife and need never touch the surface of the wood. Because the hot knife is kept away from the finish, there is less chance of creating more damage when making the repair. Mohawk offers a special, temperature-controlled knife for melting the burn-in sticks. However, I modified my standard burn-in knife by adding a rotary, lamp-dimmer switch for controlling the temperature. Too much heat causes the melted sticks to boil, which leaves air bubbles in the repair and darkens the color.

Repairs are made in the traditional manner of flowing melted material into the damaged area, leaving a dome-like mass. Air bubbles are removed by allowing the repair to cool for 10 to 15 seconds and then pressing on the material with a fingertip dipped in Plane Balm, Mohawk's skin and finish protector. With the easy melting, flexible repair sticks, I found this step to be rarely necessary.

Leveling the Repair

To level the repair with the surrounding wood, Mohawk includes a patented device called an Ieroplane, which takes the place of a sharp chisel and allows even a novice to pare away excess material without fear of gouging the surface being repaired. The Ieroplane is a large round blade mounted in a non-marking plastic frame, as shown in the photo at left. The height of the blade relative to the repaired surface can be adjusted with a top-mounted knurled wheel. The blade is adjusted to just skim the top off the mounded repair, which should be allowed to cool four to five minutes. The Ieroplane is pushed through the repair material with a slight rolling or twisting motion. Keep adjusting the blade to take off paper thin slices until the repair is almost dead even with the surface.

If necessary, further leveling can be accomplished with Mohawk's Level Aid, which is used as naphtha would be for a conventional repair. Level Aid is applied with a felt pad, a rag or 600-grit, wet-or-dry sandpaper. Limit the sanding and smoothing to just the repair area with as little overlap onto the surrounding finish as possible.

Graining can be done with appropriately colored, fine-line artist's markers in the normal manner. Spraying lightly misted coats of lacquer until the depth and gloss of the repair's finish matches the original provides a quality repair in a minimal amount of time.

TRIMMING BURN-IN REPAIR MATERIAL FLUSH is done without fear of damaging the surrounding finish, thanks to the Ieroplane. The Ieroplane is included in Mohawk's new Concept 2000 repair system, which makes burn-in repairs easier for the beginner.

BRUSHING IN WOOD-GRAIN DETAILS puts the finishing touches on an almost invisible burn-in repair. Shellac-resin sticks melted with a hot knife fill the damaged area. Graining details help hide the repair, and a few mist coats of lacquer finish the job.

repair at least three times or until most of the excess material has been removed. But don't try to get the fill dead even with the knife because it's easy to damage the surrounding finish, especially if you don't keep the knife moving.

Leveling the Repair

When finished with the hot knife, the repair should be slightly proud of the finish. As the resin cools, it hardens almost immediately. I shave off the remaining excess filler with a chisel I hone to a razor's edge on an 8,000-grit Japanese waterstone.

After carefully cutting back the repair, you may find bubbles or unevenness. One of the characteristics of a burn-in stick that makes it such a good repair material is its forgiving nature. Just reapply heat, and the resin will liquefy again whether it's been 30 seconds or 30 years since the repair was made. This reversibility means the repair can be pulled out if you botch the job or if a better technique is developed.

The next step in the leveling process is to wipe the resin with a felt pad and a solvent to help smooth the repair, as shown in the photo on the facing page. I like to use

Brasiv (Mohawk) or VM&P naphtha. Often I use cigarette lighter fluid from Walgreen's. The lighter fluid is essentially naphtha, but the little flip-top can is a very handy dispenser, which keeps spills to a minimum.

Although they will rarely damage any cured finish at least 30 days old, solvents should be tested on an inconspicuous spot. Brasiv is fast acting, so it requires some care. Using a clean felt pad slightly moistened with solvent, I rapidly rub the repair. The solvent softens the resin, and the felt absorbs any excess material while polishing the surface smooth.

Many people use 400-grit wet-or-dry sandpaper to smooth repairs. This technique requires a very gentle touch and often creates more work if you damage the finish around the repair. I try not to use sandpaper and especially don't recommend it for beginners. Things can get out of control in a hurry, particularly on more modern pieces that have toner in the finish instead of being stained in the more traditional manner. Sanding, even with 400-grit paper, will cut through the toned finish in short order, and it is difficult to patch unless you are skilled with an airbrush. If you must use abrasives, keep in mind that a finish is not very thick, and you can sand through it in less time than it takes to talk about it. Try starting with less aggressive 600-grit paper, and use a very light touch.

Adding Wood-Grain Details

At this stage, the repair should be flat and the color close to the shade of the background wood, but it still won't look quite right. The missing ingredient is the natural grain lines of the wood. The grain lines need to be duplicated to commit what the French call trompe l'oeil, literally, to "trick the eye." Wood-grain lines of the appropriate size and color are drawn with fine-line graining pens or painted with a brush and pigments blended with lacquer and a little retarder, as shown in the photo above.

BUFFING THE REPAIR WITH SOLVENT and a felt pad softens the resin, levels it with the surrounding wood and leaves a smooth surface. Excessive resin should first be pared away with a razor-sharp chisel.

Sources

Hot Tools, Inc.
24 Tioga Way
PO Box 615
Marblehead, MA 01945
617-639-1000

**Mohawk Finishing
Products, Inc.**
Route 30 North
Amsterdam, NY 12010
518-843-1380

**Star Finishing Prod-
ucts, Inc.**
360 Shore Drive
Hinsdale, IL 60521-5822
708-654-8650

C.W. Crossen
706 East River Drive
Davenport, IA 52803
800-722-9342

**The Sanding
Catalogue**
PO Box 3737
Hickory, NC 28603-3737
800-228-0000

Artist's pens and pigments also can be used and offer an even greater selection of colors.

For best results, be sure to follow the natural grain lines. Run the pen lines past the edges of the repair, and avoid hard edges. Smooth in coloring pens and brushed colors with your finger to blur the lines. These grain lines are vital to an invisible repair, so take the time needed to get them right.

Getting the Finish Right

Though the repair is now smooth, grained and color-matched, it will probably still stand out. The sticks leave glossy repairs, so the sheen of the repair won't match the surrounding wood's sheen. The location of the repair and the finish of the piece determine the next step.

In most situations, the gloss of the repair can be adjusted with either Burn-In Seal (Mohawk) or Sheen (Star) aerosol lacquers. These aerosol lacquers are specifically formulated to reduce the gloss of the burn-in repair to match most wood finishes. I am not sure how they work, but they sure do the job. I lightly mist on several coats of the lacquer until the repair blends in with the rest of the finish. If necessary, you can topcoat with the original finish for a perfect match.

This technique works fine in most situations. One problem area, however, is tabletops, particularly those with a high-gloss finish. A high-gloss finish works like a mirror, reflecting light and accentuating scratches, nicks, and even repairs.

Repairs to these finishes are a compromise, and no technique yields perfect results. With that idea clearly in mind, I like to use MicroMesh Abrasives, available from C.W. Crossen (see Sources at right), to reproduce the luster of a high-gloss finish. These superfine abrasives, available in grits as fine as optical grade (12,000 grit) are worked with a drop or two of water from the finest grits downward toward the coarser grades, which is the reverse of the usual procedure, until a reasonable duplication of the surrounding sheen is achieved.

ROBERT JUDD is a professional furniture repairer and refinisher in Canton, Mass.

Credits

The articles in this book appeared in the following issues of *Fine Woodworking*:

p. 4: Making Sense of Sandpaper by Strother Purdy, issue 125. Photos by Strother Purdy, courtesy *Fine Woodworking*, © The Taunton Press, Inc.; Drawing by Tim Langenderfer, courtesy *Fine Woodworking*, © The Taunton Press, Inc.

p. 10: Sanding in Stages by Gary Straub, issue 99. Photos by Susan Kahn courtesy *Fine Woodworking*, © The Taunton Press, Inc.

p. 18: Surface Prep: Why Sanding Isn't Enough by Philip C. Lowe, issue 152. Photos by Asa Christiana, courtesy *Fine Woodworking*, © The Taunton Press, Inc. except photo on p. 18 by Michael Pekovich, courtesy *Fine Woodworking*, © The Taunton Press, Inc.

p. 22: Mix Your Own Oil Stains by Thomas E. Wisshack, issue 110. Photos by Vincent Laurence, courtesy *Fine Woodworking*, © The Taunton Press, Inc.

p. 26: Glazes and Toners Add Color and Depth by David E. Colglazier, issue 116. Photos by Alec Waters, courtesy *Fine Woodworking*, © The Taunton Press, Inc.; Drawing by Heather Lambert, courtesy *Fine Woodworking*, © The Taunton Press, Inc.

p. 32: Dry Brushing Wood Stains by Roland Johnson, issue 123. Photos by Aimé Fraser, courtesy *Fine Woodworking*, © The Taunton Press, Inc.

p. 37: Fuming with Ammonia by Kevin Rodel, issue 126. Photos by Scott Phillips, courtesy *Fine Woodworking*, © The Taunton Press, Inc. except photos on p. 37 by Dennis Griggs, courtesy *Fine Woodworking*, © The Taunton Press, Inc.

p. 42: How to Match a Finish by Jeff Jewitt, issue 148. Photos by William Duckworth, courtesy *Fine Woodworking*, © The Taunton Press, Inc.; Drawing by Heather Lambert, courtesy *Fine Woodworking*, © The Taunton Press, Inc.

p. 47: A True Oil Finish by Chris Becksvoort, issue 152. Photos by Erika Marks, courtesy *Fine Woodworking*, © The Taunton Press, Inc.

p. 50: A Hand-Rubbed Oil Finish by Thomas E. Wisshack, issue 97. Photos by Vincent Laurence, courtesy *Fine Woodworking*, © The Taunton Press, Inc.

p. 55: An Easy, Durable Finish by Lon Schleining, issue 154. Photos by Mark Schofield, courtesy *Fine Woodworking*, © The Taunton Press, Inc.

p. 60: Choosing and Using Brushes by David Sorg, issue 156. Photos by Mark Schofield, courtesy *Fine Woodworking*, © The Taunton Press, Inc. except photos on p. 63 (center, right top and right middle) by Kelly Dunton, courtesy *Fine Woodworking*, © The Taunton Press, Inc.; Drawing by Kelly Dunton, courtesy *Fine Woodworking*, © The Taunton Press, Inc.

p. 68: Making a Case for Varnish by Frank Pollaro, issue 117. Photos by Vincent Laurence, courtesy *Fine Woodworking*, © The Taunton Press, Inc.

p. 74: Garrett Hack by David E. Colglazier, issue 122. Photos by Vincent Laurence, courtesy *Fine Woodworking*, © The Taunton Press, Inc.

p. 80: Wiped-On Varnish by Thomas E. Wisshack, issue 132. Photos by Jefferson Kolle, courtesy *Fine Woodworking*, © The Taunton Press, Inc.

p. 87: A No-Brainer Varnish Technique by Jeff Jewitt, issue 143. Photos by Susan Jewitt, courtesy *Fine Woodworking*, © The Taunton Press, Inc. (except photo on p. 89, bottom right, courtesy *Fine Woodworking*, © The Taunton Press, Inc.)

p. 91: Padding Lacquer by Mario Rodriguez, issue 118. Photos by Vincent Laurence, courtesy *Fine Woodworking*, © The Taunton Press, Inc.

p. 96: Padding on Shellac by Jeff Jewitt, issue 112. Photos by Charley Robinson, courtesy *Fine Woodworking*, © The Taunton Press, Inc.; Drawing by Michael Gellatly, courtesy *Fine Woodworking*, © The Taunton Press, Inc.

p. 101: A Traditional French Polish by Sean Clarke, issue 155. Photos by Mark Schofield, courtesy *Fine Woodworking*, © The Taunton Press, Inc.

p. 109: A Short Course in Gilding by Stuart M. Altshuler, issue 142. Photos by Jonathan Binzen, courtesy *Fine Woodworking*, © The Taunton Press, Inc.

p. 114: Milk Paint by Mike Dunbar, issue 136. Photos by Mike Pekovich, courtesy *Fine Woodworking*, © The Taunton Press, Inc. except photo on p. 115 by Matthew Teague, courtesy *Fine Woodworking*, © The Taunton Press, Inc.

p. 120: Three Finishes for Birds-Eye Maple by Teri Masaschi, issue 163. Photos by Mark Schofield, courtesy *Fine Woodworking*, © The Taunton Press, Inc.

p. 125: Creating an Antique Painted Finish by Kirt Kirkpatrick, issue 120. Photos by Vincent Laurence, courtesy *Fine Woodworking*, © The Taunton Press, Inc.

p. 129: Finishing Mahogany by Jeff Jewitt, issue 164. Photos by William Duckworth, courtesy *Fine Woodworking*, © The Taunton Press, Inc.

p. 136: Making Wood Look Old by Jeff Jewitt, issue 127. Photos by William Duckworth, courtesy *Fine Woodworking*, © The Taunton Press, Inc.

p. 141: Repairing a Worn Finish Without Refinishing by Pinchas Wasserman, issue 128. Photos by William Duckworth, courtesy *Fine Woodworking*, © The Taunton Press, Inc.

p. 144: Burning In Invisible Repairs by Robert Judd, issue 102. Photos by Charley Robinson, courtesy *Fine Woodworking*, © The Taunton Press, Inc.

The New Best of Fine Woodworking series

A collection of the best articles from the last ten years of Fine Woodworking.

OTHER BOOKS IN THE SERIES

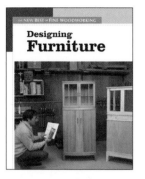

Designing Furniture
The New Best of
Fine Woodworking
From the editors of FWW
ISBN 1-56158-684-6
Product #070767
$17.95

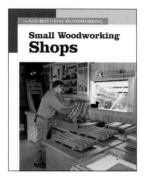

Small Woodworking Shops
The New Best of
Fine Woodworking
From the editors of FWW
ISBN 1-56158-686-2
Product #070768
$17.95

Working with Routers
The New Best of
Fine Woodworking
From the editors of FWW
ISBN 1-56158-685-4
Product #070769
$17.95

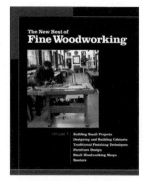

The New Best of Fine Woodworking Slipcase Set Volume 1

Designing Furniture
Working with Routers
Small Woodworking Shops
Designing and Building Cabinets
Building Small Projects
Traditional Finishing Techniques

From the editors of FWW
ISBN 1-56158-736-2
Product #070808
$85.00

Designing and Building Cabinets
The New Best of
Fine Woodworking
From the editors of FWW
ISBN 1-56158-732-X
Product #070792
$17.95

Building Small Projects
The New Best of
Fine Woodworking
From the editors of FWW
ISBN 1-56158-684-6
Product #070767
$17.95